PROBLEMS AND PERSPECTIVES IN HISTORY

EDITOR: H. F. KEARNEY MA PHD

Greek Thought and the Rise of Christianity

A list of titles in the
PROBLEMS AND PERSPECTIVES IN HISTORY series
will be found on the back cover of this book

Greek Thought and the Rise of Christianity

James Shiel

LECTURER IN CLASSICAL AND MEDIEVAL STUDIES
AT THE UNIVERSITY OF SUSSEX

BARNES & NOBLE, Inc.
NEW YORK
PUBLISHERS & BOOKSELLERS SINCE 1873

Published in the United States in 1968
by Barnes & Noble, Inc.
105 Fifth Avenue, New York

Editor's Foreword

'Study problems in preference to periods' was the excellent advice given by Lord Acton in his inaugural lecture at Cambridge. To accept it is one thing, to put it into practice is another. In fact, in both schools and universities the teaching of history, in depth, is often hindered by certain difficulties of a technical nature, chiefly to do with the availability of sources. In this respect, history tends to be badly off in comparison with literature or the sciences. The historical equivalents of set texts, readings or experiments, in which the student is encouraged to use his own mind, are the so-called 'special periods'. If these are to be fruitful, the student must be encouraged to deal in his own way with the problems raised by historical documents and the historiography of the issues in question and he must be made aware of the wider perspectives of history. Thus, if the enclosure movement of the sixteenth century is studied, the student might examine the historiographical explanations stretching from More's *Utopia* and Cobbett to Beresford's *Lost Villages of England*. At the same time he might also be dealing with selected documents raising important problems. Finally he might be encouraged to realize the problems of peasantries at other periods of time, including Russia and China in the nineteenth and twentieth centuries. In this particular instance, thanks to Tawney and Power, *Tudor Economic Documents*, the history teacher is comparatively well off. For other special periods the situation is much more difficult. If, however, the study of history is to encourage the development of the critical faculties as well as the memory, this approach offers the best hope. The object of this series is to go some way towards meeting these difficulties.

The general plan of each volume in the series will be similar, with a threefold approach from aspects of historiography, documents and editorial consideration of wider issues, though the structure and balance between the three aspects may vary.

A broad view is being taken of the limits of history. Political history will not be excluded, but a good deal of emphasis will be placed on economic, intellectual and social history. The idea has in fact grown out of the experience of a group of historians at the University of Sussex, where the student is encouraged to investigate the frontier areas between his own and related disciplines.

H. KEARNEY

for
Hugh Kearney

ΕΙΣ ΧΑΡΙΝ

Contents

CONTENTS

PART TWO

Historical Approaches to the Synthesis

Acknowledgements

We are grateful to the following for permission to reproduce copyright material:

George Allen & Unwin Ltd for material from Nietzsche, *Beyond Good and Evil* and *Human, All–Too–Human*, trans. H. Zimmern, and *The Will to Power*, trans. A. M. Ludovici; Troeltsch, *The Social Teaching of the Christian Churches*, trans. Olive Wyon, and *My Life and Thought* by Albert Schweitzer. The Trustees of the British Museum for material translated by Dr J. Shiel from *Fragments of an Unknown Gospel and other Early Christian Papyri*, by H. I. Bell and T. C. Skeat. Cambridge University Press for material from *Pagan and Christian in an Age of Anxiety* by E. R. Dodds. Harper & Row, Publishers, for material from *The Influence of Greek Ideas on Christianity* by E. Hatch (Harper Torch Book, N.Y., 1957). Lawrence & Wishart Ltd and International Publishers Co. Inc., New York, for material from F. Engels, *Introduction* (London 1895) to Karl Marx, *The Class Struggles in France 1848–50* (English translation, London 1934). Oxford University Press for material from *A Study of History, Vols. 5 and 7* by Professor A. J. Toynbee. The author for material from *Judaism and Christianity* by The Rev. Dr. J. W. Parkes. A. D. Peters & Co. for material from 'Arnold Toynbee's Millennium', by Professor H. R. Trevor-Roper, printed in *Encounter*, June 1957, Vol. VIII, No. 6. Russell & Russell, Publishers, for material from *Foundations of Christianity* by Karl Kautsky, trans. Henry F. Mins. Routledge & Kegan Paul Ltd and the Bollingen Foundation for material from *Collected Works of C. G. Jung, Vol. II, Psychology and Religion: West and East*, trans. R. F. C. Hull; Bollingen Series XX.11; copyright by Bollingen Foundation, New York, 1958; distributed by Pantheon Books. Routledge & Kegan Paul Ltd and Humanities Press Inc. for material from *Outlines of the History of Greek Philosophy* by Eduard Zeller, trans. L. K. Palmer. The Viking Press, Inc., for material from *The Portable Nietzsche*, trans. and edited by Walter Kaufmann, copyright 1954 by The Viking Press, Inc.

Part One

The Problem

The student of Greek thought wonders what to make of the New Testament. The book is printed in the same Greek alphabet as his other texts, and he is aware that among papyrus discoveries fragments of this book have appeared alongside those of the pagan Greek literature, written in the same style of handwriting and obviously belonging to the same ancient world. Yet when he attempts to read this document of the ancient mind he is surprised. Its style of expression is not that of the Greek he knows. It feels rather like a veneer of Greek over a Semitic mode of expression. Though the book deals with wisdom and morality he sees little hope of finding in it the congenial and lucid thoughts of the Greek thinkers. And that little hope will vanish if he happens to notice in Saint Paul's letters a severe warning against Greek philosophy as a dangerous deception.[1]*

If from here he moves forward to the Christian Greek writing of only a few generations later he comes upon a reversed situation. The religious message is now framed in philosopher's language, reminiscent at every turn of Heraclitus or Plato or Aristotle or Cleanthes or Epictetus. Indeed, the Christian religion is now occasionally called a philosophy and its founder described as a philosopher. One Christian bishop, Phileas, on trial before the Roman magistrate Cucianus in A.D. 303, says that Paul himself was the greatest of the Greeks and a finer philosopher than Plato.[2]

This 'conversion' to philosophy entices historical exploration. At once it evokes questions and conjectures. Was Jesus of Nazareth, despite the idiom of these New Testament documents, a philosopher, belonging to the same category as the Greeks? If not, how did his message come later to be formulated in their idiom? Was there some hidden affinity between the two diverse elements? Did the rationalist thought of pagan Greece conceal a religious undertone? Or was there a philosophic element latent in the alien Semitic faith? If not, was the primitive faith deliberately distorted and pushed into an Hellenic frame? Did some economic or political factor affect the change? The educated Greek philosophers belonged to the upper classes of the imperialist

* References are to the Documentary Notes which follow.

society in which the religion of Jesus had to make its career, and eventually the historic moment arrived when these classes, and their whole political structure, were absorbed into Christianity. Is the dramatic change of idiom, then, from Semitic to Hellenic, merely the symptom of that even more dramatic social change?

For the Greeks the word 'history' meant such questioning. To the modern European mind the word also means 'story'. Questions can only be raised in the light of the actual happenings. So we must first try to sketch the basic story of the encounter, appending a few specimens of the documentary context on which both story and questions rely.

DOCUMENTARY NOTES

I

The New Testament attitude may be illustrated by a single verse from St Paul:

Take care that no one comes to take you captive by the empty deception of philosophy, based on a man-made tradition of teaching concerning the elements of the material world, and not based on Christ.

PAUL, *Letter to the Colossians* 2. 8

2

Numerous documents of a few generations later could be cited to show Christianity expressing itself philosophically and even at times calling itself a philosophy.

Nobody can deny that our Saviour and Lord was a philosopher and a truly pious man, no imposter or magician.

EUSEBIUS, *Demonstration of the Gospel* 3. 6. 8 (PG 22. 225)

Paul . . . supreme among the Greeks . . . surpassed Plato and the other philosophers.

Apologia of Phileas (Papyrus Bodmer XX, ed. Martin. Geneva, 1964)

Those who say that philosophy took its origin from the devil should recall that saying of the Scripture about the devil 'changed into an angel of light', his intention being to utter prophecy. When he prophesies in the guise of an angel of light he must tell the truth. His utterance of angelic and enlightened teaching is therefore salutary – at the particular time, that is, when he changes to this activity and not during his usual state of apostasy. He has to make use of truth to lead on the enquirer cunningly into friendship with himself and so eventually into error. . . . Philosophy, then, is not false, for the thief and liar changes his whole operation to make use of it. We are not far off the mark if we repeat the common thought that everything needful and profitable for life comes from God, and that indeed philosophy has been given to the Greeks as their own kind of Covenant, their foundation for the philosophy of Christ, even if Greek philosophers do close their ears to the Christian truth, despising its barbarian accent. . . . The philosophy of the Greeks, partial and particular though it is, contains the basic elements of that genuine and perfect knowledge which is higher than human, which is engaged upon purely intellectual objects, even upon those spiritual objects which eye had not seen nor ear heard nor the heart of man ever conceived until they were made plain to us Christians by our Great Teacher. . . .

CLEMENT of Alexandria, *Miscellanies* 6. 8 (*PG* 9. 288*)

Everything that has ever been well expressed or conceived by the philosophers or lawmakers they have elaborated . . . because of some share in the *logos*. Since of course they did not acquire complete knowledge of the *logos*, which is Christ, they often contradicted one another.

JUSTIN, *Apology* 2. 10 (*PG* 6. 460)

The divergence of these attitudes is antithetic and suggests a dramatic historical change. To probe it the historian may follow the genetic sequence of Greek rational thought, looking for any traces in it of kinship with religious belief, and then likewise survey the rise of Christian faith to detect the presence or absence there of an inner affinity with philosophy.

* Migne, *Patrologia Graeca*, vol. 9, col. 288.

I

Greek Rationalism

A glance at any literary product of the Greek mind evokes the feeling that its generative source was a love of precision. We notice at once the tendency to define and analyse. Even thought itself must be analysed into parts. There is always emphasis on measure and number and limit. The writers are ever conscious of aim and scope. They feel they must scan and define the rhythm of even the most elusive process.

The surviving written evidence of Greek philosophy presents to us an intellectual movement evolving in the direction of an ever more precise rationalism. The process begins with Thales of Miletus (c. 580 B.C.) and his effort to see beyond primitive attitudes to the cosmic mystery that surrounds the little area of human control. Thales and his successors in the cities and islands of Ionia, that meeting-place of East and West, speculated about the living stuff of the universe, more like physicists than philosophers. They thought of water or fire or some nameless vital element as dominating the cosmic process.

One Ionian, Heraclitus (c. 500 B.C.), formulated the theory of universal change, 'all things flow', a physical doctrine not exactly consoling to the human desire for a philosophy of stability.[1] Another thinker, Pythagoras (c. 530 B.C.), emigrated from the Ionian island of Samos to the Greek settlements of southern Italy and there with the initiative of genius he turned away from physical theorizing to mathematical study. His concentration on geometrical problems was a well-spring for the whole European current of progressive rationalism and science. There arose at once a fruitful tension between physics and mathematics, and from it came the monism of Parmenides (c. 500 B.C.), asserting, against Heraclitus, that, according to the logic learnt from mathematics, physical motion is impossible and its appearance an illusion. The question had thus turned to query the validity of human sensation and knowledge.[2]

Then there appeared on the scene of European history the political experiment of the city of Athens, which in the span of a lifetime came to dominate the Greek-speaking peoples of the Mediterranean world. Athens rose to military supremacy after defeating a massive Persian invasion in 479 B.C. Commercial and cultural success soon followed.

4

Urban life developed, with leisure for cultural exchange and discussion. The philosophers from Ionia and Italy came here to find a congenial forum. The result was the crop of Athenian intellectuals known as Sophists,[3] impressive examples being Gorgias and Protagoras. Among the Sophists emerged the fascinating personality of Socrates (executed in 399 B.C.). Turning away from physical theory and mathematics, Socrates devoted his attention to the human person, thus giving a new ethical turn to the course of Greek thought. Though he wrote nothing, his magisterial spirit of relentless enquiry and perhaps much of his actual words were incarnated in the dramatic writings of his devout follower, Plato (427–347 B.C.). The real fecundity of Socratic thought comes to light in whole schools of different emphasis which arose out of it.[4]

Plato founded his Academy, a fraternity of research exploring the suprasensible idea-forms, which, manifested particularly in mathematics, seemed to be eternal and to transcend the material condition of Heraclitean flux. Plato appears more intellectualist than Socrates, though ethical interests still absorb him, for his supreme preoccupation remains the Socratic 'therapy of the soul'.[5]

Plato's most brilliant pupil, Aristotle (384–322 B.C.), developed along an even more scientific line. Coming to abandon his master's principle of transcendent idea-forms he set up as his aim the scientific analysis of empirical reality. His school in Athens, the Lyceum, was a sort of scientific laboratory, empirical and rationalist in method.[6]

Other post-Socratic schools, Stoics, Epicureans and Cynics, retained the Socratic emphasis on ethical interests. The later school of the Sceptics, tired of ethical dogmatism, revived the pre-Socratic problem of perception and knowledge and advanced the method of systematic doubt.[7] The interests of these schools flowed back into the Platonic Academy, which went through various phases, dogmatic and sceptic, before developing into the movement known as Neoplatonism, which is associated with the name of Plotinus (A.D. 205–270). Though religious and mystical in outlook, Neoplatonism recalled the rationalist interests of all the earlier schools of thought.[8]

The characteristic note of all this development was a growing reliance on independent reason, a devotion to logical precision, progressing from myth to *logos*. Rationalism permeated the whole social and cultural development so conspicuous in the age of Pericles. Architecture by then had developed from primitive cultic considerations to sophisticated mathematical norms; sculpture escaped from temple image to a new love of naturalism and proportion; medicine leapt from witch-doctoring to case books; political life proceeded from tyranny to rational experiment in democracy. From practical rules of thumb geometry moved forward in the direction of the impressive Euclidean synthesis. So too philosophy made its way from 'sayings of the wise' to the Aristotelian logic, and made men rely on their own observation and reflection in facing the unexplained vastness of the cosmos.[9]

Traditional rites and taboos and attitudes were gradually undermined. Drama, for example, had begun as worship of Dionysos; its original religious quality is evident in Aeschylus with his gigantic superhuman figures. In Sophocles, human and divine are apparent, but the main interest is in the human dimension. Euripides, though not accurately described as a rationalist *tout simple*, certainly reveals scepticism about established cults. In politics there is a similar development: the Athenians became over-confident of their own rational capacities and undertook imperialist exploits beyond their resources. This excessive reliance on human endowment must have appeared to the traditional religious mind as a sin of insolence (*hybris*). The historian Thucydides apparently regarded neglect of traditional morality and social values as the prime cause of political disaster. To the conservative mind it seemed that reason (*logos*) had become too much aware of its power, too little of its limitations in practice (*ergon*).[10]

The confidence that rational explanation of phenomena could rid men of anxiety, cleansing their lives from superstitious dread, from fear of posthumous divine judgement, or of disease and death here on earth – this confidence animated the Epicurean philosophy and finally inspired the Latin Hellenist, Lucretius, into writing a poetic gospel of rationalism. Reason, said the Epicurean, could triumph over human ills by means of science, by studying 'the nature of things'. Religion, so he claimed, had arisen as primitive man's instinctive reply to fears aroused by danger without or projected by imagination within. But religion had only produced further terrors through superstition and priestcraft. Man's ultimate consolation in trouble could only come from his own power of scientific reason. Reason could formulate a conscious pattern of human perfection and could then elaborate a systematic procedure to achieve it. This had inspired the agnostic humanism of the Sophists, who wanted to turn away from theology and to concentrate on human perfection through education. The urge to elaborate a rational human paradigm and then seek to train men according to it seems to some scholars to have pervaded all Greek culture; poets, artists, statesmen and philosophers seemed to concur in making their work a training (*paideia*) for the realization of a human ideal rationally ascertained. The Latins inherited this Greek ideal, calling it *humanitas*, paying reverence and admiration to a logical pattern of human existence, wherein the humanist could find a substitute for religious faith.

So we may suggest rationalism as the typical mark of Greek achievement. Humanism is observable not just where we most expect it, in philosophic writings, but also in the great poetic creations of epic and tragedy which are the prime manifestations of the Greek genius. Humanist techniques are admirably suggested by the common Greek word, *logos*, whose connotations embrace word, thought, speech, discussion, mathematical calculation, proportion, dramatic utterance, public oration, treatise and, for the philosophers, the all-pervasive 'thinking' that fashions the cosmos and the human animal within it.[11]

Two books which epitomize the rationalism of the Greeks are the *Elements* of Euclid and the *Organon* of Aristotle. Both portray the Greek belief in systematic perfection, the ideal of Pythagoras. Both works became almost sacred texts in later Greek tradition. In the Neoplatonic schools they attracted more voluminous commentaries than any other writing, all with the purpose of raising the studious mind to the pinnacle of Plotinian contemplation. The Neoplatonist Proclus, in his devout commentary on Euclid, speaks of mathematical objects as images (*eikones*) of the supreme divine. But it is evident that minds raised on such mathematical imagery would lose all devotion to the less rational ikons of popular religion. Religious fervour had changed into scholarship.

One turns to Greek rationalism as a unique vantage point from which to view the evolution of the European mind towards civilization. The historical documents that survive show clearly a breaking away from primitive attitudes into progress and elementary science, from myths into disciplined acquisition of knowledge about the universe. The reader notices a movement away from the ancient static religions towards a more dynamic human ideal, towards an exploratory 'religion of humanity'. The philosopher's mind was less and less disposed to accept any ritual allegiances which tied him to city or nation or sect and separated him from the rest of mankind. Philosophy therefore seemed a way of purifying the religious instinct and of converting it to more universalist allegiance. Philosophy sought to be independent of any revelation that was tied to particular time and place, to be free from the institutions which transmit such revelation, free from the assent paid to it. Philosophy limited itself to experience and inference. Its progress meant that speculative interest expanded from the merely local to the universal, for the strength and attraction of philosophy is its reliance on a human faculty which is not the privilege of any caste or group or elite, the catholic endowment of reason. The history of Greek philosophy records that progress over several generations.

DOCUMENTARY NOTES

I

Because of the fragmentary state of the extant quotations it is difficult to illustrate briefly how the greatest of the Ionian philosophers, Heraclitus, confronted the central problem of the early physicists, that of movement. Indeed it is a central puzzle of all Greek philosophy that cosmic motion or vital process proves opaque to the perception of intellect. Intellect has no genuine awareness of change. Heraclitus therefore tends to pass beyond logic. But the intellectual Greeks found his words unclear and irrational, for he was almost mystical in his utterances.

This universe, the same for all, was made by neither god nor man. It ever was, ever is and ever shall be a perpetual vital fire, lighting in its measures and going out in its measures.

HERACLITUS, *fragment* 30

The main lines of Heraclitus's thought are these.
    All things are composed out of flame and resolved into it. All things come into being according to fate and everything that exists is held together through the play of contrary forces. . . . Fire is the basic element and all things are an exchange for fire, produced by rarity and density.
    But Heraclitus is obscure in all his statements.
    Everything comes to be according to opposition and all things are in flux like a river. . . . The urge in opposites towards generation he calls war or strife, the urge which leads to destruction he calls harmony and peace; change is a way up and a way down, and according to it the world is made. As fire condenses it becomes moist and constitutes water, and water when solidified is turned into earth. That is what he means by the way down. The reverse process is that when earth dissolves

8

it becomes water, and so on with the rest, for he makes all things arise like a sea vapour. This is the way up.

DIOGENES LAERTIUS, *Lives of the Philosophers* 9. 7

2

Philosophy tried to escape from the awkward notion of perpetual flux, towards something not subject to the empire of time and change. A doctrine more congenial to philosophic reason and expression soon took the field, a doctrine of intellectual stability, inaugurating the long dynasty of thought which weds philosophy to eternity, rejecting movement and physical flux as unreal shadows. Thus a monist position was reached.

We have said enough to understand the mind of the old philosophers who said that the elements of nature are multiple. But there were some thinkers who spoke of the universe as though its nature were a single unity, though they were not all unanimous either in accuracy of statement or in conformity with nature. So they have nothing to contribute to our present discussion of causation. For they speak differently from some of the physicists who do posit a unity of Being but then go on to generate things from this unity as if the unity were matter, and who assume motion as well as unity, for they have to generate the universe. But these monists say that unity is immovable. Still this much of their doctrine is relevant to our investigation of causes. Parmenides seemed to have caught the idea of a logical unity, but Melissos that of a material unity; and that is why Parmenides says the unity is finite, and Melissos that it is infinite. Xenophanes was really the first of the Monists to talk about a unity, for Parmenides is said to have been his pupil. But Xenophanes made no clear statement and he does not seem to have envisaged either a unity of definition or a unity of matter. Looking at the cosmos as a whole he said that Unity is God.

ARISTOTLE, *Metaphysics* 986 b 9

Parmenides contends, and writes it in verse to drive home his argument, that since word and idea are stable their object also is stable: it is unchanging and one.

Thought and being are the same. Thought and that for the sake of which thought is are the same. For you will never find thought without the existent in regard to which it is expressed. Nothing exists or will exist outside of being, since Destiny bound all being into remaining immobile. What mortals have set up as true conviction, statements that there is generation and destruction, existence and non-existence, change of place, change of bright colour, all this is mere names.

PARMENIDES, *Fragments* 5d, 7d

Zeno replied: Yes, Socrates, this book of mine certainly helps out the argument of Parmenides against those who try to confute him by saying that if the One alone exists many absurd and contradictory consequences follow. My work is against those who affirm plurality, and it gets its own back with interest. I try to establish that their hypothesis of a plurality of things, if one were to pursue it thoroughly, falls prey to even more ridiculous results than that of the One. Such was the contentious spirit that drove me to write this book when I was young. Somebody stole my copy after I had written it, and so the decision whether it should see the light or not was taken out of my hands.

PLATO, *Parmenides* 128b

3

The Sophists were the great rationalists, rejecting all but human concerns, measuring everything with the slide-rule of reason, teaching that even society is subject to technique.

Protagoras began one of his works with these words: 'Man is the measure of all things, the measure of what exists and the measure of what does not exist.' . . .

He commenced another work like this: 'About the gods I have no knowledge as to whether they exist or do not exist. There are many obstacles to such knowledge, for instance, the obscurity of the subject and the shortness of human life.'

Because of this opening statement he was banished by the Athenians. They burned his books in the agora after an official had collected them from their owners.

DIOGENES LAERTIUS, *Lives* 9. 51

4

Socrates devoted himself to the study of man. But he worked by rational methods and so he may rank as the founder of ethical science, measuring human action by concept and ratiocination.

Socrates was an excellent searcher after definition. He wanted to argue syllogistically, and definition is the basis of syllogism. We can justly credit Socrates with two achievements, inductive logic and universal definition, both of which are at the foundation of scientific certainty.

ARISTOTLE, *Metaphysics* M.4, 1078 b 23

5

Plato is attacked by Nietzsche for being the arch-rationalist. He advances from the principle of Parmenides that perfection of thought demands perfection of object; the object of thought (form) exists eternally outside the sense world, and since the mind is endowed with thought this must happen by remembrance of an extra-temporal pre-existence. The man who can summon up that eternal realm is a philosopher. Mathematical study offers the best training for philosophic recollection, which is the supreme human endowment. The philosopher will not be upset by the imperfections of earthly society nor elated by human works of art for his mind can view an ideal Thought and Art of perfect harmony and proportion.

Philosophers are those with the capacity to contact that which is eternally the same. . . . But men who cannot do this and wander amid the multiple objects of change are not philosophers.

PLATO, *Republic* 6. 484b

After these philosophies (Pythagoreans and Eleatic monists) came the work of Plato, who in many respects imitated them but still had many details different from the Italian philosophy. As a young man Plato was acquainted with Kratylos and the doctrine of Herakleitos which said that all sensible objects are in continual flux and that there can be no knowledge of them. This doctrine Plato retained in later life. But since Socrates concentrated on ethics and not on external nature, though in ethics he sought the universal and was the first to set his mind to definitions, Plato followed him and came to the conclusion that definitions apply to objects other than those of sense. This was his reason: it seemed impossible that the universal definition should apply to sense objects which are always changing. And so Plato called the objects of definition 'ideas', claiming that all sense-objects are related to them and named after them.

ARISTOTLE, *Metaphysics* A.6, 987a

The common vulgar opinion about knowledge is to the effect that it lacks strength or command or authority. People do not think of it as having such qualities. A man, they think, may often possess knowledge and it does not rule him; something else does, perhaps anger, or pleasure, or pain, or love, or, as often as not, fear. They think of knowledge as a slave dragged about by all the rest. Now, Protagoras, is this also your opinion? Or do you not rather think that knowledge is beautiful and, as some might say, that it dominates a man? Isn't it true that if a man can discern good objects from bad nothing can ever bully him into acting otherwise than as knowledge dictates, and its wisdom will be enough to help him?

My opinion, said Protagoras, is exactly like yours, Socrates. As much as any man alive I would be ashamed ever to deny that wisdom and knowledge are the mightiest of human things.

PLATO, *Protagoras* 352b

Since all nature is cognate and the soul has already learnt everything there is nothing to prevent a man from proceeding from the remembrance (*anamnesis*) – or, as people say, the knowledge – of one thing to the discovery of all other things, provided the man is brave and does not tire in his search.

PLATO, *Meno* 81d

The sense of sight has, in my opinion, been of the greatest utility to man. . . . For the vision of night and day, of the months, of the recurrence and symmetries and seasons of the year, has produced our knowledge of number, our notion of time, and our study of the nature of the universe. From these we have derived the type of knowledge called philosophy, and nothing better than philosophy has ever come or will ever come to mortal men as gift from the gods.

PLATO, *Timaeus* 47a

Perhaps, I said, the society we have been describing is laid up in heaven as a pattern which he who wishes can contemplate in founding the city of his own self. But it does not matter whether it now exists or ever will exist. This is the only state whose politics the philosopher can share.

PLATO, *Republic* 592b

I suppose God wanted to be the Real Maker of the essential bed and not just a particular carpenter turning out a particular bed. So he decided to make the essential nature of bed unique.
I imagine so.
So then, could we not give him some name like Maker of the Nature of things?
It would be a fitting name, for the bed and everything he makes is an ultimate natural reality.
And the carpenter? Isn't it true that he constructs a bed by craft?
Yes.
And the artist? Does he make or construct beds by craft?
Neither.
What does he do then?
I think we might say precisely that he produces a copy of what the other two make.
Right, said I. Then the artist's imitation is three moves away from natural reality, isn't it?
It is.
The tragic poet, then, if his art is imitation, is third in right of succession to the throne of truth. And the same holds for all artists.
I think so.

PLATO, *Republic* 597d

6

The scientific attitude finds its most impressive Greek exponent in Aristotle.

In the science of nature he was the most vigorous investigator of causes: he would not let the slightest detail go without accounting for it. He therefore compiled a large number of notebooks on nature.

DIOGENES LAERTIUS, *Lives of the Philosophers* 5. 32

7

Of the post-Aristotelian schools the Epicureans laid most emphasis on science as humanist panacea. Religion seemed to them a product of primitive terror that ought to give way to a rational view of nature, an atomic theory of the cosmos, man's only way of reaching a calm attitude to misfortune and death.

A person has no way of resolving fear about ultimate concerns if he is ignorant of the nature of the universe and lives in fear of some piece of mythology. That is why it is impossible to enjoy pure pleasures without the study of nature.

EPICURUS, *Chief Maxims* (quoted by Diogenes Laertius, 10. 143)

Perpetual drinking bouts and revels, the enjoyment of boys and women, the savouring of fish and everything else a rich table provides, these will not produce a happy life. It will come rather from sober calculation, searching out the reasons for every choice and every rejection, while banishing all beliefs that cause most disturbance in the soul.

EPICURUS, *Letter to Menoikeus* (quoted by Diogenes Laertius, 10. 132)

8

The Neoplatonists managed to combine rationalist tendencies with religious ones. Despite their preoccupation with oracles, theurgy and magic, the Greek habit of precise definition and analysis did not desert them. They were boldly intellectual even as regards the kinetic aspect of reality where intuition might have seemed more appropriate than logic. So we find that Plotinus does not neglect the intellectual heritage of earlier thought, and his emphasis on spirit and eternity does not prevent him from working out a theory of time.

In his writing Plotinus was concise and profound, brief, excessive in thought rather than in word. He often rises to inspiration and speaks from his own feeling rather than from tradition. Yet in his treatises Stoic and Peripatetic doctrines are embedded below the surface, and the essence of Aristotle's *Metaphysics* is there. He was never in the dark about any theorem of geometry or arithmetic, and the same was true of mechanics, optics and music, though he did not set out to promote these disciplines. In his meetings commentaries were read out, of

Platonists like Severus, Kronios, Noumenios, Gaios or Attikos, and the Peripatetic writings of Aspasios, Alexander, Adrastos or any others that were at hand. But he borrowed nothing straight out of these writings. He was original and independent in his mental work.

PORPHYRY, *Life of Plotinus* 14

We must not regard time as being outside of Soul, any more than eternity outside of real Being. Time is not an accompaniment nor a consequent of Soul. It is manifested in Soul, inheres in it, is one with it, just as eternity in real Being. We must understand the time-process (*physis*), then, as the progressive expanse of the soul's life. It advances in even and similar mutations that escape notice, and its action is of continuous duration.

PLOTINUS, *Enneads* 3. 7. 11–12

To Plotinus's exalted clarity of thought Porphyry his pupil fitted precise expression.

Some philosophers cover up their most ineffable thoughts in obscurity of style, as poets do with myths. But Porphyry regarded clarity of mind as an excellent medicine and once he had tasted and tested it he described it in writing and published it. . . . Plotinus, because of his heaven-dwelling soul and his oblique and puzzling style, seemed difficult and hard to listen to. But Porphyry was like a chain of Hermes let down from heaven to men, for with his manifold education he could make every explanation comprehensible and lucid.

EUNAPIUS, *Lives of the Philosophers* 456

9

The rationalism of the philosophers affected all sections of Athenian culture. Even Pericles was said to have been a pupil of Anaxagoras.

Socrates. It is only fair to say, Phaedrus, that Pericles was the most accomplished man in the art of rhetoric.
Phaedrus. Why?

Socrates. All the greatest of the arts call for fluency of thought and discussion about nature's loftiest things. That seems to be how a man may
gain sublimity and the capacity for all-round perfection. Now Pericles,
alongside the fact that he was gifted by nature, possessed this experience.
For I believe that when he happened upon Anaxagoras, a man with
the qualities mentioned, he became full of lofty views, and gained an
insight into the nature of mind and thought, about which Anaxagoras
discoursed profusely. From this experience he drew what was useful
for the art of public speaking.

PLATO, *Phaedrus* 269e

10

*Pericles is said to have defended Anaxagoras in court when he was charged
with impiety over his unorthodox statement that the sun is a red-hot mass of
metal. The questioning methods of the Sophists about traditional cults may
be detected in the plays of Euripides who was also listed among the pupils of
Anaxagoras.*

Nurse. . . . We have now seen the best of persons – against their will
admittedly – fall prey to evil desire. Aphrodite has proved to be no
goddess. It took something more than a goddess to inflict such disaster
on Phaedra here, and on me, and on the royal family. . . .
Phaedra. . . . Often before now in the long hours of the night I have
puzzled over the countless ways in which the lives of human beings are
degraded. I believe that their growth in evil does not come from anything innate in their mind. Many of them in fact have the gift of wise
thought. But this is the way to look at it: we humans are able to understand and grasp what is good, but we fail to work it out in action.
Sometimes this is because of sloth and sometimes because we put some
pleasure before noble action; and pleasures are many.

EURIPIDES, *Hippolytus* 358–83

11

*We do not have to read many documents to feel the essential quality of the
Greek genius, the spirit of precision, lo gran disio dell' eccellenza. Everything, even life itself, must submit to sharp analysis and definition and induction.*

Observation and calculation are expected to produce a blue-print for human action and happiness. There is assumed to be an ideal of humanity which can be rationally ascertained. Therefore the work of reasoning is man's supreme function: the philosophic life is the ultimate morality and fulfilment. The philosophers recur to the conviction that thought alone is endowed with duration and is prior to movement. Their intellectualist attitude is well summed up by the last of the great pagan thinkers when he says that action is only a weak version of contemplation.

We shall always find that action or making is either a weakening of contemplation or a side-effect of it: a weakening if the person finds no end-product other than the action; a side-effect if he has some product to contemplate better than the action itself. For why should a person who is able to contemplate the true ever go after what is only an image of the true? Backward children are a good illustration of what I mean; they are unable to manage learning and contemplation, and so they tend towards crafts and activities.

PLOTINUS, *Enneads* 3. 8. 4

17

II

Its Religious Roots

Such is our first and dominant historical impression. Yet, we must add that though Greek philosophy was a logical-geometric development, an unemotional and objective rationalism, its history shows that it nevertheless had permanent roots in the non-rational. It was abstract thought, but it had a *base pathétique*, and its characteristic rationalism was never severed from the emotive language of the *polis*, from rhetoric and drama and poetry. The same society which produced Euclid and the *Organon* produced the Eleusinian mysteries and the *Bacchae* of Euripides. Indeed the first beginnings of speculative thought seem to have had root in Dionysiac rites merging into Orphic and Pythagorean cults. A suggestion of philosophic analysis (*moira, nemesis*) is even visible in the primitive religious language. The light of reason, therefore, dawned out of the 'formless darkness' of theurgy and magic.

Furthermore, it would be wrong to assume that with the rise of rationalist philosophy and its consolation of tranquillity (*ataraxia*), Greek religious sentiment and ritual came to an end. The philosophers, despite their universalist tendencies, were a minority. They were of the educated upper-class elite, remote from the masses and the slaves. This was so in the various Hellenic city states, and it remained so after the brilliant military campaign of Alexander the Great left in its wake Greek-speaking communities all over the Near East, and later still when these were politically united into one universal *polis*, the Roman Empire. Upper-class culture never replaced popular religion. Ancient life, both social and individual, was permeated by religion to an extent the modern pagan can scarcely understand. There were local cults of immemorial antiquity, gods and shrines of field and stream and city. Crafts and occupations had their tutelary deities, and even the professional and artisan guilds (*collegia*) of the Roman Empire held their business meetings to the accompaniment of religious image and prayer. Families worshipped ancestors and retained their relics.

Men's enthusiasm could always be captured by religious propaganda, a fact which politicians and military leaders did not overlook. The Roman Emperors, beginning with Augustus, tried to channel religious sentiment into the conservation of empire and citizenship. Augustus shrewdly kept for himself the office of *pontifex maximus*, president of the ancient *collegium* of priests. But efficient political use of religion was always hampered by the profusion of local cults with which magistrates dared not interfere. The Emperors took the line of conserving and even resuscitating local observances, but an image of the goddess Roma or of the Emperor was often tactfully inserted alongside the native gods; sometimes the local god was successfully given a Latin name or identified with a Roman deity. But it cannot be said that Rome-worship or Emperor-worship ever came near to drawing all the peoples of empire into a single allegiance and enthusiasm. The best ecumenism that could be achieved was a tolerant federation; the Pantheon attempted to be a shrine for all known types of worship. But new types constantly appeared on the imperial horizon. The provinces of the East brought in fresh varieties of cult and mystery to be sampled in initiation alongside the established mysteries of Apollo at Delphi or Demeter at Eleusis or Artemis at Ephesus. The exotic Mithras came in to join Dionysos, and Osiris migrated from the Orontes to the Tiber. Religion became much the same everywhere, with just a difference of divine names.

Such adaptability was, perhaps, a virtue in the imperial religion, which also enjoyed the strength of long and venerable tradition, the attraction of art and ceremony, the popular appeal of oracle and theophany. But it did not encourage a spirit of enquiry, it did not build up a rational morality, it was tainted by superstition and fear of the after-life, it lacked the cohesion of monotheism. In spite of such weaknesses it attracted philosophic defenders like Plutarch and the Neoplatonists. Under the rational influence both of philosophy, which dealt in generalities and world views, and of the socially united *orbis*, religious sentiment tended to become universalized and world-conscious, no longer limited to the preservation of *polis* or tribe. But the cults lacked overall cohesion and impetus. Political revolutions had made the Mediterranean world a mixture of peoples who were united by Roman domination without acquiring a unity of conscience or social harmony through the enthusiastic sharing of a single religious ideal. The ancient national religions were too narrow and closed for a universal society, and not one of the mystery cults which emerged and gained ground from them was able to replace the others definitively.

It would have been very strange if philosophy had managed to carry even the elite few completely clear of such pervasive religiosity. Philosophy and all the other departments of rationalist *paideia* could not sever themselves from their social substructure. We have noted that in fact religious interests first prompted philosophic ones.[1] The ascetic cult of the Orphics preaching salvation through a liberation of the soul from its material prison is at the root of the Platonic dualism. Pythagoras, lauded as the first pure mathematician, was yet an ascetic, and his community of followers constituted one of the most persistent religious traditions in the ancient world.[2] The Ionian physicists described the vital principle of all things as divine, even though for them it was a material principle. Socrates was too humble a man to condemn the religious rites by which the common folk about him were fortified. Indeed he himself was said to have received his philosophic vocation from the oracular priests of Delphi. His intuitive genius gave him more than merely conceptual knowledge. It gave him an agnostic penetration beyond concept and external technique. A lot of Socrates's energy went into showing that sophistic conceptualizations were in fact inadequate. His inner penetration controlled his whole personality and activity so completely that the surprising statement 'virtue is knowledge' seems rational in the light of it. Philosophy, a perpetual process of enquiry and criticism, was the raft to which he entrusted his own spiritual voyage, but he did not deny that the gods might have other vehicles for other men. He opposed the smug scepticism of the Sophists. It is a tragic irony that after all this he was charged in court with having promoted agnosticism and caused neglect of the established religion. Though as a philosopher he was resigned to the thought that death might be a final extinction, Plato shows him entertaining his prison visitors by devising proofs for the immortality of the soul. His urbane jest at the actual point of death spoke of it as Apollo's moment of healing. After Socrates, religion could never again be strictly limited to emotive ceremony and initiation but would suggest intellectual quest. Unlike other founder mystics, Socrates left behind him an intelligentsia rather than a church. Nevertheless he was essentially a religious man.[3]

Inevitably his greatest pupil shared his religious spirit. Plato is never far away from the language of the Eleusinian mysteries, aware that the deepest truth cannot be formulated logically but emerges through a sort of initiation experience in the soul. The non-initiated are as ineffectual in achieving it as those condemned in Hades to carry water in a sieve. But the initiated find that the sun shines even into the dark of the temple, for in the shadowy cave of earthly life they alone have the purity to discern the truths of the suprasensible world. Plato is in fact the inventor of the term 'theology'. He seems to anticipate something like the Christian problem of faith and reason when he visualizes a

harmony between the rational and irrational elements in human personality. He also urges against the Sophists that practical wisdom is
impossible without a theoretical approach to 'the unconditional': 'God
is the measure of all things.'

Apparently sensing a danger in systematic intellectual formulae, he
liked to leave questions open, only hinting at lines of advance through
imaginative stories; as he says, 'through images' (di'eikonōn), likenesses
and shadows of the Real. He thus professes faith in the open future of
human knowledge. His use of images in essaying philosophic truth is
imitated by Plotinus. It suggests that the ultimate truth is not a matter
for proof, *quod erat demonstrandum*, but for intuition.[4]

With Aristotle religious notions tend to fade into the background
of empiricism, but it is also true that the surviving fragments of his
early dialogues reflect Plato's religious attitudes and that these remain
operative in all Aristotle's later works. He retained the Platonic name
theologia for his 'first philosophy', and his ethical ideal, despite his
empiricism, remained the training of the mind towards contemplation
(*theoria*), suggesting that the philosophic pattern of life must be somehow 'made divine'. This view of human knowledge superseding mortality animated later Greek science. Its abiding European inspiration is
abundantly evident in the fact that the medieval Brunetto Latini in
his *Tesoro* was to resurrect from the newly translated *Nicomachean
Ethics* and pass on as bread of life to his pupil Dante the ideal of man
achieving divinity through intellectual endeavour (*come l'uomo
s'eterna*). Thus the empirical rationalist Aristotle did not leave religion
on one side as an opium of the people, deriving at best a merely pragmatic truth from their 'will to believe', but actually regarded philosophy
as a rational approach to the religious realm. The highest human
truth remained for him, and so for later tradition, the Platonic *aeterna
veritas*.[5]

Religious notions also affect the post-Aristotelian schools. The
Epicureans, strange though it may sound, were in practice an exemplary
community of ascetics.[6] The Stoics had as central tenet the notion of
divine providence, and thought of man cooperating freely with God
for the achievement of God's unknown purpose.[7] They urged men to
abandon all things external and seek only goodness (*aretē*) within the
soul. They also thought of God's providence as uniting all things by a
certain cosmic inter-awareness: wherever man helped man he was
actually a divine agent (*deus est mortali mortalem iuvare*). Cicero retains
and passes to Latin posterity the Platonic notion of philosophy as more

than a humanist rationalism: it is 'the knowledge of both human and divine things'.

The Cynics were popular religious preachers and vendors of pamphlets, or else they were hermits like Diogenes. Though the post-Platonic schools tended to be materialist there came a spiritual revival of Platonism with Plotinus. The later Neoplatonist thinkers, however, deviated far from the Socratic type of spirituality, losing themselves in the techniques of the Pantheon, in divination, oracle-collecting and theurgy, considering themselves as priests.

A strange fusion of Stoic, Platonic and Pythagorean ideas into Oriental religious practice is evident in the Hermetic books which appeared from about the middle of the first century onwards. They show the sort of syncretism of thought and religion that had been going on for a generation or so before the Christian era. Philosophy was no longer a matter of pure rationalism; it was just an aid to religious sentiment, inculcating the deification of man through Gnosis.[8]

The Neopythagoreans who decorated their underground chapel in Rome in the age of Claudius religiously allegorized scenes from Homer into their wall-paintings. Odysseus tied to his mast to escape the Sirens of pleasure is the model of the philosopher in his voyage of escape from the disturbance of the world.

Such philosophic allegorizing, a technique for rendering primitive epics intellectually respectable, was fostered by the Greek schools. These schools also tended to make philosophy a tool for rhetoric. Rhetoric as employed by men like Cicero was not without political efficacy, but under the Empire, where political deliberation was less necessary, it declined into ceremonial and theatrical declamation. Philosophy became scholastic, reduced to classroom reading of passages and commenting on them. The discourses of Epictetus and the later sophistic biographies show us the philosophic schoolroom in action. Original minds were critical of this scholasticism but could do little to change it.

The whole population of the Roman *orbis* was so much in the grip of religious fears and hopes that philosophy had little chance of shaking itself free from belief. It became spiritualized. Philosophers studied religion and religious men studied philosophy. A remarkable instance is the first-century Jew, Philo of Alexandria, who sought to produce a synthesis out of the sacred stories of the Jewish Bible and Greek philosophy. His key concept was the Stoic *logos*, which he used as equivalent for the Jewish 'Word' or 'Wisdom', which in some texts comes close to being a secondary God. Philo equated this Wisdom with the Platonic–Stoic cosmic reason. His other great borrowing from the Greeks was allegoric explanation: Jacob's stone pillow, for instance, could be interpreted as an incorporeal intelligence making contact with Jacob's head.[9]

An indication of the religious motive permeating Greek philosophy is the fact that right at the end of antiquity it was an 'exhortation to the philosophic life', written by Cicero in imitation of a previous one by Aristotle, the *Protreptikos*, which first turned Saint Augustine's thoughts towards Christianity, and then it was a reading of Plotinus which took him a stage further towards the spirituality of Saint Paul.[10]

So, then, Greek philosophy, this impressive product of rationalist endeavour, can be viewed as a flowering in the religious field. However rationalistic the philosophic method, there always remained certain common ground between philosophy and religion. As we have seen, in the whole course of Greek philosophy it was apparently only the Sophists like Protagoras whose humanism was, like modern humanism, agnostic.

Later Greek philosophy tried to assume the essential function of religion whereby the creative urge of emotion and imagination devises symbols to safeguard day-to-day action from the petrifying menace of inevitable failure and final extinction. Philosophers sought to console and support men against loss, illness, bereavement, death; this 'consolation' theme is found in Cicero, Seneca, Plutarch, Porphyry and Boethius. It has affected the whole European tradition. Even a modern philosopher like Bertrand Russell aims at a 'conquest of happiness', at creating through philosophic imagination a more bearable world than that of mortal experience, in a thought-construct that holds some of the beauty of tragedy. This is not far from a religious aim.[11] The philosopher's joy lies in a state of mind, an occupation of thought. For the saint, on the other hand, all growth of mind is growth in prayer; his ideal is an 'elevation of the soul to God'. But both philosopher and saint find joy in mental activity, and this stimulates expression, moving from intensive to extensive, from unity to multiplicity. Their modes of expression often coincide, for both philosopher and saint share themes such as truth, God, the heavens, the soul, good and evil, humanity. Even the most primitive religion necessarily includes elements of philosophy, for it implies a certain attitude of mind towards ultimate concerns such as the secret of the universe and the menace of death.

Nevertheless, there is an ultimate gap between philosophic activity and any religion which can be termed historical. The philosopher looks for universal values in his present human experience. He borrows no deity from the historical past: to become a philosopher he does not have to face an 'historical problem': he has no gap to bridge between the god or saint of the dead past and the self of the living present; he needs no subtle theology to demonstrate how some divine person who once acted or lived visibly on earth may still be operative upon it in an invisible way. The philosopher does not try to build a bridge of devotion or ritual towards any other historical personage. His consolation resides within his own thought, and is not a personal relationship but a form of knowledge, a *gnosis*. Such was the Greek philosopher. For him the aim of philosophy was to discover the order of the cosmos, an order which he conceived to be eternal and immutable. It is difficult to imagine how he would ever take to the idea of a personal God who could intervene arbitrarily in cosmic events. It is this opposition between Greek *logos* and historical occurrence, between objective logic and personal relationship, between immutable order and divine initiative, that is uppermost in our mind when we turn to observe the confrontation of Greek philosophy with nascent Christianity.

DOCUMENTARY NOTES

I

However much we may come to admire the rational illumination of Greek thought we do well to review the darker side of its development, for philosophy grew out of primitive religious attitudes and permanently retained traces of them. Seen in this way it may look less antithetic to the faith which later took possession of it.

The early Ionians are manifestly close to primitive religious modes of thought. Philosophy had not yet quite differentiated itself into an independent discipline. The early 'physicists' were far from scientific: they were rather 'wise men' who did little to verify their theories by experiment.

According to Plato Thales was one of the seven wise men. He was the first to receive the name of Sage, when Damasias was archon in Athens and all seven sages received their name.

DIOGENES LAERTIUS, *Lives of the Philosophers* I. 22

Some thinkers have said that the soul is mingled with the whole universe. Perhaps that is the origin of the saying of Thales that all things are full of gods.

ARISTOTLE, *De Anima* 405 a 19

2

The Pythagoreans have a distinctly religious background to their mathematics.

Pythagoras of Samos . . . went to Egypt and became a student of their religion and was the first to bring the rest of philosophy to the Greeks. He showed a more conspicuous devotion than anyone else as regards sacrifices and services in temples.

ISOCRATES, *Busiris* 28

Thales was a Phoenician, and was said to have met the prophets of Egypt, and Pythagoras too met the Egyptian priests, who circumcised him so that he could enter their inner shrines and learn their mystic philosophy.

CLEMENT of Alexandria, *Miscellanies* 1. 15. 66 (ed. Stählin, p. 41; *PG* 8. 768)

Apollodorus the mathematician states that Pythagoras went and sacrificed oxen when he had discovered that the hypotenuse in a right-angled triangle has a square equal to the squares on the other sides.

DIOGENES LAERTIUS, *Lives of the Philosophers* 8. 12

3

Socrates, though he may be credited with the invention of philosophic definition, yet mistrusted dogmatic and definitive formulae. He used concept only to refute conceptual dogmatism: he always tried to keep arguments moving and rarely advanced convictions of his own. Intuition seemed to have been a greater force in his religious life than logic.

My method of enquiry has raised up against me a great many enemies making bitter and hostile accusations. They label me for instance as a professor of wisdom. They imagine, because I happen to show that someone else does not possess a wisdom which he professes, that I myself must possess that particular wisdom. But the truth of the matter is this. Wisdom belongs only to God, and the statement of the oracle that I am the wisest of men only means that human wisdom is really worth very little. The god is not really referring to this Socrates here; he is only borrowing my name as an illustration. As much as to say: the wisest man is the one like Socrates who realizes that in actual truth he knows nothing.

And that is why I keep going round inquiring and investigating, out of obedience to God, about anybody I think to be wise, whether he be a citizen of Athens or a stranger. And if I find that he is not wise I lend a hand to the oracle by proving that he is not. This occupation has taken so much of my time that I have none left for political life or for my private affairs. And so my obedience to God has reduced me to poverty.

PLATO, *Apology of Socrates* 22e

I have no sure knowledge about the other world. So I admit my ignorance.

Ibid. 29b

Socrates indeed went to prison after making his last utterance in the Areopagus ascribing to God alone the knowledge of the things that are hidden from us. But those who came after him, though unable to understand even earthly things, professed to understand heavenly things as plainly as if they had witnessed them. Aristotle, pretending to discern celestial matters with greater accuracy than Plato, rejected Plato's view that God exists in a fiery substance, and asserted instead that he exists in an etherial fifth element.

Unknown Author (Pseudo-Justin), *Exhortation to the Greeks* 36 (PG 6. 305)

4

Plato is a distinctly religious thinker and uses the language of the mysteries. His later works express a sort of cosmic religion. Like Socrates he senses the limits of human perception. Many of his dialogues are open-ended, stimulating to read but playing round their point and enforcing no explicit conclusion.

Adeimantus, I said, we are not poets at this moment but founders of a city. Founders to be sure must know the forms in which poets ought to make their myths and if poets transgress these forms they must be prohibited. But the founders themselves must not start myth-making.

All right, said Adeimantus, but tell me this. What are to be the correct forms for discourse-about-the-divine (*theologia*)?

Something like this, I answered. One must always speak of God as he really is, whether one is writing epic or lyric or tragedy.

That is right.

Now God is good, and as such we must describe him.

Yes.

PLATO, *Republic* 379a

Plato held that . . . sense objects are always in flux and so there can be no real knowledge of them.

ARISTOTLE, *Metaphysics* 987a

The Good has a very peculiar sort of beauty if it can provide knowledge and truth and yet is itself above these. You didn't mean to call it pleasure, I'm sure.

A dreadful idea, I said. No, this is how you must pursue the image of it.

How? he asked.

You will admit, I think, that the sun not only gives visible objects the power of being seen, but also gives them their generation and growth and nourishment. And the sun itself is not that generation.

Well?

In the same way with objects of knowledge you can say that not only the fact of their being known comes from the good but their existence and essence come from it as well. And the good is not the same as their essence; it is beyond essence, because of its superior nobility and power. My word! said Glaukon mocking me, what a heavenly superiority it has!

PLATO, *Republic* 509b

Socrates. Splendid, Timaeus. Certainly we ought to accept the story as you tell us. And now that we have heard your fine opening strains, go on and complete the melody for us.

Timaeus. Well, we must explain the reason why the composer created generation and all this universe of ours. He was good, and nothing ever causes the slightest jealousy to one who is good. Being beyond jealousy he wished all things to resemble himself as nearly as possible. One would be quite right in accepting the opinion of the wisest men that such was the supreme principle of generation and of the universal order. For the god wished that all things should be good and that as far as possible nothing should be inferior. So he took over all that was visible, all that was not at rest, all that was moving out of tune and in disorder, and he reduced it from disorder to order, thinking the latter to be by far the better state. It was not and is not admissible that the action of the best may ever be other than the finest. Consideration showed him that of the things which by nature are visible one which lacks mind will never be in all respects better than one which possesses mind; and further, that mind can never come to anything except in the company of soul. Because of this consideration he put mind into soul and soul into body and thus fashioned the universe, aiming to produce a work which would be by nature the fairest and best. And so we must use the most likely description and say that this universe is a living thing, a creature which really possesses mind, and that it came to be such through the foresight of the god.

PLATO, *Timaeus* 29e

As Pherekydes said, when the supreme god decided to make the world he had to turn himself into desire.

PROCLUS, *On the Timaeus* 32c

There is none of the radiance of justice or temperance, or the other objects precious to the soul, in their likenesses in this world. A few men penetrate through dim instruments to images of them, and contemplate the nature of the exemplar. We philosophers were able to view bright beauty herself at that time when, accompanied by Zeus or one of the other gods, amid happy chorus we saw that blessed vision, and were initiated into what we may rightly term the most blessed of the mysteries. These we celebrated in our integrity, knowing nothing of the evils which awaited us in later time, mystically viewing apparitions that were whole, simple, calm and blissful, receiving our vision in a pure ray of light, being pure ourselves, not buried in this tomb which we now carry round, this body which confines us like an oyster shell.

PLATO, *Phaedrus* 250b

At first these two horses in the soul are recalcitrant and rebellious, forced into terrible and unusual tasks. But in the end when they realize they cannot escape trouble they advance as guided, yielding and consenting to obey the charioteer's orders. Approaching their goal they catch sight of the flashing vision of the beloved. When the charioteer sees it his memory is carried towards the real nature of beauty where it stands along with temperance on a sacred pedestal. Memory trembles at the sight and falls back to the ground in adoration . . .

PLATO, *Phaedrus* 254b

Athenian. There are two points, previously explained, which lead us to belief in the gods?
Kleinias. Which ones?
Athenian. The first is what we said about the soul – that it is the noblest and divinest of all those things whose movement, when it has become generation, provides a constant stream of being. The other is the order inherent in the motion of the stars and those bodies subject to a controlling intelligence which sets the whole in order.

PLATO, *Laws* 966d

5

Aristotle's early works, dialogues in the Platonic manner, held the religious tone of his master. Later, in his more empirical years in the Lyceum, his school treatises dwelt less upon religious themes. Yet in the Ethics when he speaks of the supremacy of intellectual activity he uses a religious phrase to characterize it: science is man's way of being divine, a larger than human activity. Later Greek intellectuals were inspired by this thought.

Aristotle makes it quite clear that he envisages something transcending both mind and substance. This he does in the concluding chapters of his dialogue *On Prayer* where he distinctly says: God is either mind or something that goes beyond Mind.

SIMPLICIUS, *Commentary on Aristotle's 'On the Heavens'* 485. 19

There is a treatise of Aristotle in which he says that . . . the cosmos itself is god-possessed and is a living being, rational and immortal.

PLUTARCH, *Doctrines of the Philosophers* 5. 20

Aristotle says that Providence extends downwards only as far as the moon, but later on he turns round and says that the cosmos is God – an admission that the part which lacks God is in fact divine like the rest.

CLEMENT of Alexandria, *Exhortation* 5. 66. 4

If intellect is something divine in relation to man then the life of intellect is divine compared with human life. A human being must not, as the poets tell us, strive only for human things, nor because he is mortal attend only to mortal things, but he should pursue a divine life (*athanatizein*) to the limit of his powers, striving in every way to live according to the best element within him.

ARISTOTLE, *Nicomachean Ethics* 1077 b 30

I know that I am mortal and the creature of a day. Yet when I study the clustered wheeling of the stars I no longer touch earth with my feet, but with Zeus himself I am filled with the elixir that makes the immortals.

PTOLEMY the Astronomer, *Epigram* (*Anthologia Palatina* 9. 577)

Euclid sought with precision for the acute Mind in immortal figures, and for all the properties that blossoming Nature intended for shapes and magnitudes. This work he placed as foundation-stone of all wisdom, and left to the universe a token of his brilliance.

Verse written in Arethas's Euclid (Bodleian MS D'Orville 301, f.307v) (A.D. 888)

6

The Epicureans had a rather confused notion of scientific method. Sense perception was their ultimate criterion, but where sense perception could not easily be used as verification, as in theories of the heavenly bodies, they were happy enough with a plurality of divergent hypotheses. They held on to a religious notion of the knowing mind penetrating cosmic space, forgetting their materialist premise that mind could not survive outside of its bodily envelope. Obviously they were influenced by more primitive views. In any case their science is completely subordinate to ethics. They are not atheistic: their gods, the finest atomic structures in the cosmos, live remote from human cares, like Aristotle's First Mover.

A feature of scientific enquiry (*historia*) is this: striving for knowledge about rising or setting or solstice or eclipse or other such phenomenon can contribute nothing to human happiness, and people who are expert on these matters can still be subject to vain fears. . . .

If we come to the conclusion that a celestial phenomenon is accounted for in one particular way but yet observe that there exists quite a variety of explanations we shall be just as free from anxiety by accepting these many as by holding to our own single explanation.

EPICURUS, *Letter to Herodotus* (Diogenes Laertius, 10. 79–81)

First of all hold that God is a living being, immortal and blissful, for such is the common conception of mankind. And do not attribute to him anything alien to his immortality or not consonant with his bliss.

EPICURUS, *Letter to Menoikeus* (in Diogenes Laertius, 10. 122)

As Antisthenes says in his *Physics*, there are many gods according to law but only one according to nature.

PHILODEMUS, *On Piety*, ed. Gomperz, p. 72

7

The Stoics also have a theology, with ethical interests predominating. The culmination of their science of nature is in fact the theory of 'natural law' and the inter-awareness (sympatheia) of all parts of the cosmos. Socially motivated by the universal Empire, they were the first among the ancient thinkers to emphasize the universal brotherhood of man.

The Stoics hold that the universe has two principles, one active, the other passive. The passive one is matter, the substance that lacks all quality, and the active is the reason that inheres in matter, that is to say, God. God is everlasting and makes by his art all individual things through the whole extent of matter. . . .

God, Nous, Fate, Zeus: these are all one, and there are many other divine names besides. At first God turned all substance through air into water. And as in animal reproduction seed has its container, so God as seminal reason of the universe is contained in the moist element, making matter adaptable for the creation that is to follow. . . .

They think of God as living, immortal, rational, perfect or intellectual in his happiness, admitting no evil in his nature, exercising providence over the universe and its parts. But their conception is not anthropomorphic. God is called artificer and as it were father of all things, either all of him or that part of him which extends through everything and according to its powers is denoted by many names.

DIOGENES LAERTIUS, *Lives of the Philosophers* 7. 134–6, 147

Living according to excellence is the same thing as living by experience of natural events, as Chrysippos says in his first book *On Ends*. Our human nature is part of the universal nature. Therefore the end is to live according to nature, which means living according to one's own nature and that of the universe. We must practise nothing that is normally forbidden by nature's common law, that right reason which moves through all things and is identical with the god who is head of the administration of the universe.

DIOGENES LAERTIUS, *Lives of the Philosophers* 7. 87

8

In the Hermetic and Gnostic writings we find philosophic elements, such as the nous *of Anaxagoras, mingling with creation myths and popular superstition.*

God Nous, being male–female, being life and light, gave birth by reason to another demiurge Nous, who as god of fire and spirit fashioned seven governors who enclose in circles the sensible universe; their government is called fate.

Corpus Hermeticum 1. 1. 9

Nous, father of all, being life and light, brought forth Man, equal to himself, whom he loved as his own child. For he was very beautiful, having the likeness of his father. In all truth God was enamoured of his own image and handed over to his offspring all the tasks of creation.

Corpus Hermeticum 1. 1. 12

But in another way the Gnostics make the beings of the Beyond seem impure. When they compose incantations as if addressing these beings, not just Soul but the beings beyond Soul, what else can they mean except that the heavenly beings are subject to men and must follow their orders when they utter magical formulae and spells and enticings, provided there is somebody possessing a little of the technique of uttering such verses and rhymes and breathings and hissings, which are supposed to have power over the world Beyond? If this is not what they mean they must explain to us how unbodied beings are affected by sound. Persons who make their spells take on a sacred appearance seem to forget that they are detracting from the sacred character of those beings.

PLOTINUS, *Enneads* 2. 9. 14

9

Philo combines traditional biblical story with Greek idea by means of allegory.

'And the angels (*Hebrew text*: sons) of God seeing the daughters of men, that they were beautiful, took to themselves wives, choosing from among them all' (*Septuagint, Genesis* 6. 2).

Moses has the habit of giving the name 'angels' to what other philosophers call 'spirits' (*daimones*), meaning souls which fly in the air.

Nobody must think that the statement is just myth. Necessity demands that the cosmos be full of soul throughout, each part containing living beings that fit it and benefit it, earth having land animals, sea and river having water animals, fire having igneous animals (by all accounts Macedonia breeds most of these), and the heavens having the stars. The stars are souls, undefiled throughout and divine, and so they move in a circle, the movement which is most akin to mind, and the mind in each of them is of the purest. Necessarily, then, the air is full of living things, though to us these are invisible, just as air itself is invisible to the bodily eye.

PHILO, *On the Giants* 2. 6

IO

Among these companions at that unsteady age I was studying works of rhetoric, the art in which I wanted to shine, for my ambition was damnable and puffed up, being a mere delight in earthly vanity. And in the course of reading I came upon a work of Cicero, whose style, if not his heart, wins general admiration. The work contains his exhortation to philosophy and its title is *Hortensius*. Now this book changed my feelings, turned my prayers towards you, Lord, and left my aims and desires different from before. Every vain ambition suddenly seemed cheap to me, and I began to desire the immortality of wisdom with an incredible fervour of heart. And I began to rise and return to you.

AUGUSTINE, *Confessions* 3. 4

But then when I read those books of the Platonists I was taught by them to seek incorporeal truth, and so I saw your 'invisible things, understood by the things that are made'.

AUGUSTINE, *Confessions* 7. 20

Plotinus, called by the ancients theiotatos (*most divine*) *is probably the most spiritual philosopher in history. True, he does not see history as a drama of divine episodes with a beginning in time, but he sees the world permeated by spirit, the lower orders of being emanating from the higher in a direction opposite to that now conceived as evolution. Emanation, like evolution, does not need supernaturalist dualism. The destiny of soul is to return and become spirit. This ultimate fusion of self in the All, which seems more Oriental than Greek, is not to be induced by any of the cults or initiations or sacraments so favoured by later Neoplatonists. Plotinus favours instead an inner prayer of* nisus *in the soul, awaiting the action of the divine.*

In this oracle of Apollo Plotinus is described as good and simple, gentle and charming. This was our own impression of him too. The oracle adds that he was ever wide-awake, keeping his soul in a pure state, ever straining towards the divine which he desired with his whole self. He made every effort to get free and rise out of the bitter wave of bloodthirsty life here below. This god-like man often lifted himself towards the first god, the god beyond, by means of meditations and the ways traced by Plato in the *Symposium*. And that god who has neither shape nor conception, established above intellect and concept, became manifest to him. And I too, Porphyry, declare that on one

34

occasion I drew near and was united with the same god, when I was in my sixty-eighth year.

PORPHYRY, *Life of Plotinus* 23

If the One is of such a nature as we have described how did It come to have any derivative hypostasis, of plurality or dyad or number, instead of remaining by itself? Why did it overflow into the multiplicity which we notice in things and which we try to refer back to the One? The matter may be explained only on condition that we first call upon God himself, not uttering any loud-sounding formula but tensing ourselves within our soul into prayer towards him; this is the way to pray as single one to single One.

PLOTINUS, *Enneads* 5. 1. 6

Abandoning all things without, a man must turn round towards the inner reality, and not incline to any of the things outside. He must ignore all externals, first by a proper disposition of mind and later by ignoring the forms of things, ignoring even himself to arrive at the vision of that Object. After becoming one with it and after holding fit converse with it he must return, if this is possible, to announce to others the union there. Maybe Minos experienced such union, for he was called 'friend of Zeus'; remembering the experience he made laws as images of it, inspired in his legislation by contact with the divine. But if a man thinks that political matters are beneath him he may remain Above: this would happen to anybody with much experience of the vision. For God, as our Teacher tells us, is exterior to no man; he is present in all though they are unaware of it. It is they themselves who run away from him; rather they run away from themselves. They cannot take hold of that from which they have fled, and if they have fled from themselves they cannot look for another; just as a child, if his mind is deranged out of all self-recognition, cannot recognize his father, whereas a person who comes to know himself will also know his origin.

PLOTINUS, *Enneads* 6. 9. 7

If only a man can be aware of this union with the Supreme he possesses in himself an image of it. And if from there he could cross over as image to archetype he would reach the goal of his journey. As he falls away from the vision, he will rouse up the power within and will know himself perfectly ordered, and he will cease to be weighted down, and will rise through virtue to Mind and through its wisdom to the Supreme. This is the life of gods and of godly happy men, a release from things here to things There, a life with no pleasure here below, a flight of single one to single One.

PLOTINUS, *Enneads* 6. 9. 11

In brief, our answer to the problem of evil is this: evil does not come from God nor from any other one single cause. No one agent deliberately brings it into existence. One cannot introduce a Form of evil things, and Matter cannot be suggested as their cause either. The forms are all of the divine intellect and they regulate essences or essential perfections; and matter, too, comes from God, for it is necessary to the universe. . . . We must think of evils then as having neither a formal nor a material cause; as Plato says, they are the unintended outcome of partial and diverse causes.

PROCLUS, *On Plato's Republic*, ed. Kroll, Teubner, p. 37, 24

I I

For the best minds of antiquity philosophy and its attendant mathematics had a religious quality. It was ultimate. It provided the man of intellect with the inner assurance which other men sought in mystery cults. Its rational quality satisfied the mind and the ascetic exercise it involved resembled religious devotion. From the point of view of either intellect or religion it was the supreme product of the pagan world.

Let us see how this science extends right from the most elementary notions to the most final ones. Timaeus calls mathematics the Path of Knowledge. Mathematics bears the same relation to universal knowledge and first philosophy as education does to moral excellence. The one equips the soul with permanent habits for the perfect life, the other prepares the intelligence and the eye of the soul for a turning round from things here. In the *Republic* Socrates is right in saying that the eye of the soul blinded and wounded by other pursuits can be given its light again only by mathematics. It can be aroused once more to the vision of being, carried from images to true objects, drawn from dark-ness into the light of intellect, taken from the dark cave, the chains of becoming and the shackles of matter, into bodiless and indivisible reality. For the beauty and order of mathematical relations and the durable stability of contemplating them joins us fixedly with those intelligible objects which ever endure, ever shine with divine beauty, ever preserve their mutual order. . . .

Where then and by what means does the man of philosophic nature come to this birth of intellectual knowledge, this awakening to real existence and to truth? He is motivated by an incompleteness of inher-ent principle. His native virtue lacks complete vision and technique, and the man of such nature is aroused of himself and charmed towards the real. But then, as Plotinus says, he needs mathematics to accustom him to incorporeal reality. By use of mathematical models he may be brought to notions of dialectic and to the contemplation of real exist-ents.

Mathematical science then clearly confers the most basic of all con-tributions to philosophy. We should look at this more in detail. In the realm of theology it prepares application of intellect. In the truth about the gods there are truths which appear difficult and steep to the imperfect of understanding, but mathematical reasonings, through their images, leave them trustworthy and clear and final. For these reasonings show up in number the reflection of super-substantial individualities and reveal the superior power of spiritual forms through these mathematical forms that we are able to grasp. So Plato teaches us many splendid doctrines about the gods by means of mathematical forms . . .

PROCLUS, *On the First Book of Euclid's Elements*, ed. Friedlein, Teubner, pp. 20–1 ›

The philosopher as priest of the God who is over all things must abstain from flesh meat and always strive to come near to God, solitary to solitary.

PORPHYRY, *On Abstinence*, ed. Nauck, Teubner, 176, 9

The philosopher must above all be able to recognize the unnecessary, regarding self-sufficiency to be the greatest of riches.

PORPHYRY, *To Marcella*, ed. Nauck, Teubner, 292, 18

If in a final glance back over the development of Greek thought we discern, like the ancient historian Diogenes Laertius, two main currents, we might say that one of these, the Ionian, was an emphasis on external nature. The most forceful representative we saw of this physical philosophy was Heraclitus. After him came the pluralists, Empedocles and Anaxagoras, and the atomists Leucippus and Democritus. This stream of thought runs in the direction of empirical science rather than religious belief: it is dominated by sensation and matter.

But if we may make a final generalization, it was the other current, the Italian, with its emphasis on inner contemplation and mathematics, that had the greater influence. Pythagoras had concentrated on mathematical norms and prepared for the Monist logic of Xenophanes, Zeno and Parmenides, which was to make a central contribution to the thought of Plato. And if we are going to think of later centuries it is hard to resist Whitehead's phrase, 'a series of footnotes to Plato'.

The keynote of Platonic philosophy is the eternal stability of idea. Idea, says the Platonist, is a datum independent of the human brain. Indeed all human thinking is but a carving along joints of reality that are eternally pre-existent (Phaedrus, 265e). Analysis and synthesis follow cadres of thought already at our disposal. The design of thought is fixed before we think: its laws are given, and creative novelty is repugnant. There is more in the fixity of eternity than in temporal movement; at best movement can be only a 'mobile image' of such fixity. Here Platonism verges on an otherworldliness where the twin qualities of Greek thought, mathematical precision and religious inspiration, blend into a theology. Since movement implies a 'fall' and diminution of stability God must be absolutely stable. But this God of pure idea could have little appeal outside the social circle of an intellectual elite. This 'Thought of Thought' is too remote from the stress and mobility of real life and has little in common with any gods to whom mankind has ever prayed, with any cosmic power addressed personally as You, least of all with 'the God of Abraham, Isaac and Jacob'.

III

The Rise of Christian Faith

A great religious movement can usually be traced back historically to the crisis of one extraordinary person, facing, out of a moment of solitary intuition, divergent lanes of effort for his own life: the one path easy, the other difficult; the one familiar, the other unknown; the one comforted by a given company of society, the other lonely. He sees on the one hand possibility of personal advance, of possession, of rewarding effort in the tasks of his society. He sees on the other the inner meaning of religious ideas in his tradition: perhaps an idea of the vanity of earthly achievement, or the difficulty of moral integrity, religious practice being moral preservative or remedy, or the prospect of confident death, immortality and reward. In the illumination and impulsion of the moment he decides inwardly. And this decision once made clarifies all subsequent choices and opportunities and the organization of effort, first his own, then that of followers. But behind all the later social development lies that original solitary experience.

If the historian is to have more than surface understanding of the vast cultural and social complex known as Christianity he must try, whatever the difficulties, to discern its prime creative decision.

In this effort he encounters what is possibly history's most vexed problem, 'the quest of the historical Jesus'. Much has been written about the famous 'Socratic problem', that of distilling the philosopher's biography from its artistic embodiment in Plato's dialogues. But an even greater problem confronts the historian of Christian beginnings. Through the centuries of faith the problem did not arise, for critical history lay dormant, to be awakened only at the Renaissance. Since then the trickle of historical criticism has become a flood. From the time of Erasmus the sacred texts of primitive Christianity have been more and more subjected to the same treatment as secular documents.

As yet this process has not reached definite conclusion. The documents of Christianity have been singularly resistant to conclusive verdict and have consequently invited an extensive variety of historical opinion.

Their difficulty is basically the fact that they are 'church' documents, not meant to be biographical, but pastoral and doctrinal: 'These things are written that you may believe.' Their problematic character is reflected in a variety of factors: (*a*) the awkwardness of the language, a patois veneer of Greek overlying Semitic idiom; (*b*) the fact that three of these documents are so alike that some sort of 'copying' evidently attended their composition; (*c*) the presence of a miraculous element, conspicuously absent from the rationalist Hellenic historians; (*d*) the parables and other 'forms' of evangelical instruction; (*e*) the preoccupation of the writers with Old Testament 'fulfilment' in practically everything they write; (*f*) their preoccupation with belief and theology (Christology) rather than with a plain narrative of events.

In patristic and medieval times history respected theology as its mistress and did not seek to disturb the theological portrait which faith found in the pages of the New Testament. The critical approach of history to these documents was inspired by the Renaissance and began to trespass on the field of traditional devotion in the eighteenth century. Woolston, the English deist, depicted Jesus as a human prophet of natural religion. Voltaire saw the divinity of Jesus as an invention of the priests. Rousseau saw a Hebrew sage, counterpart to Socrates the Greek sage. Reimarus saw a political Messiah, not divine, not even prophetic. In the nineteenth century Strauss explained the Christian doctrine of divinity and miracles as a part of Jewish messianic myth retained in the new legend-creating faith. Bauer took the extreme view that Jesus never existed at all except in evangelistic imagination. Renan's famous *Vie de Jésus* (1863) pictured a rationalistic and poetic hero, a charming modern-style *homme idéal*. Weiss, with whom the problem was carried into the twentieth century, regarded Jesus as a Jewish man of his time whose preaching was inspired by the hope of achieving future Messianic status.

Harnack's celebrated *Essence of Christianity* (1900) represented Jesus as getting away from the tangle of Judaic dogmatism to stress a more rational doctrine, that of the fatherhood of God and the brotherhood of men; but this new and simple morality was later to be adulterated into mere dogma by the alien intrusion of Hellenic metaphysics. Wellhausen reacted against Harnack by showing that Jesus was not an anti-Jewish rebel but rather a Jewish teacher of the Law: 'Jesus was not a Christian – he was a Jew.' Loisy countered Harnack's ethical 'essence' in another way: by contending that later accretions, such as Church and sacraments, though not originally visualized by Jesus, were yet products of his 'Holy Spirit'; at this, however, the Roman Catholic authorities, dissatisfied with the implications of Loisy's apologetic, excommunicated him from the Church and the sacraments he had sought to defend.

A prime emphasis of Harnack and other critics was on the ethical element in the teaching of Jesus, though perhaps the emphasis was not as exclusive as some opponents of it believed. At any rate it provoked reaction from those who stressed the non-philosophic, revelational, cultic side of the teaching, arguing that Jesus could not be detached from his Jewish milieu and made into a liberal moral philosopher. The effort to enrol him in the ranks of the great philosophers was not successful.

For instance, Albert Schweitzer, like Weiss and Wellhausen, stressed that Jesus could not be detached from the current Jewish dogmatism, however irrational this might now appear to us. His apocalyptic vision expected an imminent entry of divine power and glory on the Jewish scene and a regime of Messianic deliverance, an advent so near as to leave all other human concerns futile; this eschatological hope, however, did not materialize as Jesus expected and his vision of it culminated in his execution. Schweitzer's view presupposed the hitherto unorthodox idea of an undivine Jesus 'capable of error'; but the author held that ill-fated credulity and Jewish dogmatism did not spoil the real kernel of Jesus's teaching, which is ethical and capable of universal relevance once it is extracted from the shell of either Jewish or Christian dogma.

The late-Jewish Messianic world-view is the crater from which bursts forth the flame of the eternal religion of love. . . .

The historical Jesus moves us deeply by His subordination to God. In this He stands out as greater than the Christ personality of dogma which, in compliance with the claims of Greek metaphysics, is conceived as omniscient and incapable of error.

A. SCHWEITZER, *My Life and Thought*, Allen and Unwin 1933, pp. 69, 73

Gradually, then, the notion emerged, and was stressed by Grütz-macher, that the historical canvas could not be accurately cleaned, and that all we would ever have was a faith-portrait, which could inspire Christian devotion, albeit a meagre inspiration for the rationalist historian. A 'Jesus of history' even as accurately describable as the Napoleon of history would not, it was argued, be sufficient to move men's hearts. The emphasis of the most recent critics has therefore been on faith and revelation, not on history, though they all take for granted the historical human existence of Jesus, 'a Jew in the late period of the ancient world' (Brunner). Criticism centres on the first revelational preaching (*kerygma*) and the 'forms' – parable, myth, maxim – which it adopted. Contemporary criticism finds little need to be anti-ecclesiastical or anti-dogmatic like that of Harnack, for it assumes that the *kerygma* goes on in new forms. More attention is thus paid to doctrine than to history. History, it is felt, does not give us the biography of Jesus; rather, the historical fact is the *kerygma* itself. Kerygmatic statements about Jesus as 'the Word made flesh' are outside the vision of history and belong rather to faith and theology. Modern theologians like Brunner and Barth are undisturbed if the historical personality of Jesus is not easily recognizable in their Christ of revelation; they argue that divine faith is more important than human history, that the New Testament is not interested in any historical personality. So the latest stage of the long historiographical battle with the difficulty of the early documents brings into view again the medieval faith-picture from which it all began.

Even though it is thus widely felt that an historical biography of Jesus is impossible, the tradition has not left the historian without any access to his mode of thought. Here one could be content with a minimum of easily accepted biographical fact: that Jesus was not merely a Christian 'myth' but an historical human being; that, however disputable the record of other details of his life, it is an indubitable fact of Roman history that he was executed, for endangering the peace, by Pontius Pilate, *procurator* of Judaea.[1] A general impression of his thought may emerge more clearly than details of his life.

Biographical history involves the task of criticizing the array of documents, canonized and uncanonized, heretical and orthodox, the problem of synoptic comparisons, the problem of assessing the interval of oral transmission between founder's speech and evangelist's writing. But the historian of ideas can instead take almost at random early records of the message of Jesus and feel there the lineaments of a theme. A certain religious uniformity pervades the documentary material which has survived to us from the early Christian communities, and an impressive case has been made out that this uniformity is ultimately based on words spoken by Jesus himself and on the dominant intuition behind them.

If we simply take for instance the earliest scraps of manuscript document that mention Jesus, what do we find? We find mostly collections of prophetic sayings (*logia*), which seem to have been the basis of much of the earliest Church preaching and writing. Their idiom is that of the

Jewish Rabbis. Ringing through them is an urgent announcement: there will suddenly appear in Jerusalem the 'kingdom of God'. In view of this advent all present aspirations, personal or political, are pronounced ephemeral, for the dimensions of that apparition are so mighty that they can only be adumbrated in Jewish aphorism, in simile and paradox. The kingdom is not here, though it is 'at hand'. For the present there is the Community of those 'looking out for the Kingdom', heralds of its advent. Jesus may not have defined precisely what he meant by 'at hand', but his followers, when later grouped into a Church, seem to have reflected his attitude, regarding their Church as provisional for an interim of expectation, a time for preparedness and surrender to God's design.[2]

In view of the coming Kingdom Jesus seems to have advocated a submissive readiness of spirit, a childlike trust in the divine giver of life, a reliance on giving away goods rather than on possessing them, so that life might enhance other life and be open at every moment to the powerful intervention of the fatherhood of God. Men have sensed within this a sublime and ultimate moral insight, providing remedy for personal and social problems. But it was not expressed by Jesus in ethical abstractions. It came in simple phrases and in dramatic Jewish gestures like that final one at the Passover meal, which summed up all his ethic, the broken bread denoting his own life given away to nourish others, 'my body which is given for you'.

There is growing evidence that the country in which Jesus moved was quite Hellenized.[3] Recent discovery reveals that the Essene monks were not without copies of the Bible in Greek, papyrus fragments of which were found in the seventh cave at Qumran. In the early second century commercial documents and marriage contracts, involving Jewish names, as well as some literary texts written in Greek on skin and papyrus, were in use at Murabba'at in the Judaean desert. One small fragment of these even looks like part of a Greek philosophic text. The fragments so far published are small, but at least one can notice that Greek terms like *paideia* (formation) and *physis* (nature) were familiar in this remote area, not to mention Hellenized biblical terms like *ktisis* (creation) and *pneuma* (spirit). From Capharnaum one is within sight of Greek cities such as Gerasa or Gadara where Greek savants and rhetors lectured and argued. Jesus may have walked their streets and been acquainted with their language. But it is most unlikely that he held discussions with the philosophers, for he and his followers belonged to a social class completely out of touch with theirs. His

Jewish message and idiom were addressed to the depressed social class, the *am ha-aretz*, of Galilean Judaism, not to Jews of superior class who were so conscious of their *status perfectionis*, nor to the educated Hellenists.

It is therefore the Jewish tradition rather than the Hellenic which can give some insight into the personal thoughts of Jesus. Hellenized Christianity has dressed these thoughts in another idiom, sometimes, no doubt, obscuring them. Consequently the Jewish historian is often in a better position than the Christian to understand Jesus sympathetically. Martin Buber once made a statement of dramatic sincerity about his 'Great Brother': 'We know him from within, in the impulses and stirrings of his Jewish being, in a way that remains inaccessible to the peoples submissive to him.'

The idiom of the New Testament is only superficially that of the Greek classics and tends to conceal an actuality that can only be sensed by inner awareness of Jewish religion. The teaching of Jesus falls within the spiritual tradition of the great Jewish prophets. Like them it urges a 'turning' in trust which opens up life to the possibilities of divine action.

> Jesus lived and died a Jew, and our present knowledge of Pharisaic Judaism enables us also to see that in the fundamentals of his teaching, in his message about the nature of God and man, about the kingdom of God, and about the relations of men to each other and to their Father in heaven, there is nothing which does not stem from his Jewish background or is not to be found adumbrated in Pharisaism.

JAMES PARKES, *Judaism and Christianity*, Gollancz 1948, p. 41

Where then are we to mark the first deviation from the Jewish idiom of Jesus into the Hellenic idiom of Christianity? Paul, despite the 'barbarian' detestation of Greek philosophy which we noticed at the outset, must surely rank as an archetypal Hellenizer. Critics such as Wendt, Wrede and Goguel have seen in Paul's teaching an illegitimate development of that of Jesus. Bultmann sees him as the spokesman not of Jesus but of the Hellenistic Church. Certainly in the writings of Paul and John we find modes of expression which can hardly have been those of Jesus himself. And yet the earliest parts of our Greek New Testament were written by Paul. He was a product of the sophisticated milieu of Tarsus in the province of Cilicia. Unlike a Palestinian Jew his mentality was an amalgam of two cultures, Hebraic and Greek.[4]

After his conversion fourteen years of his life were spent in Greek lands, especially in Syria and Cilicia. The Greek environment of Tarsus and of the cities where he travelled as a missionary, his intercourse with educated men, and the pervasive commerce of ideas through the Empire, meant that he was familiar with Greek modes of thought. He preached to communities of Diaspora and convert Jews, less literal in their adherence to Jewish rules than those of the Holy Land. He preached in terminology they had come to understand: they were prepared for the idea of redemption by a saviour, the idea of a god-man, the use of allegory. These Jewish communities were Hellenist. Their religious language had already been tinged with the pagan idiom of the Cynic or Stoic sermon to the crowd (*diatribē*), and their exegesis with the allegorical method of the Greek grammarians. Traces of Hellenic paganism are visible even in the Septuagint Bible, and this Greek Bible, though regarded by some Palestinian Jews as a 'sin of the golden calf', was from the start the sacred book of the Christians. The *Torah* was not always congenial to Greek Jews and Paul's preaching replaced it by belief in Jesus as Messiah risen from the dead. When Jewish opposition appeared he turned to the Gentiles. For them he advocated, against Judaean Christians, a less stringent adherence to details of the Law. The destruction of Jerusalem in A.D. 70 transferred Christian initiative from Judaea to Hellenistic lands.

Paul 'spoke and disputed with the Hellenists' (*Acts* 9. 29). In his writings new Greek connotations wrap up traditional Hebrew conceptions such as *faith, righteousness, truth, law.* Paul is no friend of Greek philosophy. Yet when facing an Athenian audience he essays to translate his message into the cultural language of the Empire, an action which the Christian Fathers justified as an 'accommodation' (*oikonomia*). Paul certainly belongs to the Hellenized Roman Empire. In a quite un-Jewish way he proclaims his Roman citizenship. Indeed, the final goal of his journeying is the capital, Rome, and in the face of trial and imprisonment his hope remains: 'I must see Rome.' After the division in the Jerusalem community between Hebrew and Hellenist Jews, the latter moved out into the Greek cities, and there was full scope for Paul's task of missionary expansion. A generation after the Galilean preaching of Jesus, the Christian mission was being directed to the Greek-speaking citizens of the Empire. Rome, which had been hated as the 'great Babylon', became, after the execution there of Peter and Paul, the sanctuary of Christian devotion, whereas Jerusalem was the holy city which drew the thoughts and tears of Jesus himself. All

Jews whether of Palestine or of the Greek-speaking Diaspora looked to Jerusalem and its Temple as the visible centre of their religious unity. But the new Christian movement, born of schism in Judaism, takes as its centre the metropolis of the Empire. Its Hellenist idiom shows in the fact that until the close of the second century the Church at Rome was Greek-speaking, set in the same background of Greek culture as the more numerous Christian communities of the East.

The essential feature of early Christianity is corporate organization. The existence of the Church is the first and inescapable fact that faces the historian. Whatever his approach to the earliest documents, even in such unlikely quarters as choosing between textual variant readings, the Church with its doctrine of Christ meets his eye. Organization is what strikes the reader at his first turning over from *Gospels* to *Acts*: he finds a 'community' with 'common property', 'breaking of bread' and 'prayers'. The organization has worship at its centre. In fact the early documents have survived because they were readings used in the Christian ritual. The writings that now make up the New Testament, 'memoirs of the Apostles' and inter-church letters, were read out in the weekly meetings and formed a distinctive addition to the traditional Greek readings from the Jewish scripture: the reported *logia* of Jesus were regarded as the divinely inspired counterpart of the ancient Torah and prophets, being in fact their 'filling-up' and true meaning. Recent scholarship has pointed out a remarkable resemblance between the basic Gospel pattern and that of the Jewish liturgical Haggadah of the Passover meal. The Christian meetings were primarily religious, not cultural or political, as comes out in the impartial enquiries of the Roman magistrate Pliny in Bithynia in the year 112 when he wrote to the Emperor Trajan about the Christians in his province (*Letters* 10. 96–7).

The strange un-Jewish fact about the new cult was that Jesus himself received divine honour. Pliny was informed that the Christians accorded worship to Jesus 'as to a god' (*quasi deo*). The Christian Church has through the centuries adhered to this doctrine of the divinity of Jesus. The doctrine was congenial enough to the Hellenic mind – so long as it appeared as a deification of man and not as the incarnation of God. The Greek word for God, *theos*, could be used with adjectival force, making it easily applicable to godly men, for instance to the deified emperors. Hellenistic Judaism, however, though prepared to expect a celestial quality in the Messiah, still thought of him as rising out of humanity. Historical doubt has therefore been raised whether Jesus ever actually described himself as God, for in his language it meant claiming to be JHWH, an impossible claim for any devout Jew, to whom JHWH was unique and utterly other-than-man, the distinct partner in a personal encounter and contract, with a proper name never reducible to adjective. The Jewish faith had stressed the non-humanity of God and the non-divinity of man. But Paul's letters offer abundant evidence that the early Christians worshipped Jesus as divine. Converts from Judaism were required to make the unprecedented gesture of paying to his name, a common Jewish personal name, the honour they had hitherto reserved for the sacred tetragrammaton which no human might pronounce. The Septuagint euphemism *kyrios* (Lord), used instead of JHWH, was now applied to Jesus. He was more than the 'anointed leader' (*mashiach;* in Septuagint Greek, *christos*) awaited by the Jews; he was divine, and as such he was worshipped.

The readings heard in the early Christian liturgical gatherings sought to justify this divine worship by reporting sayings of Jesus himself which claimed or implied his own divinity. Here the non-Christian historian is full of doubt, and suspects sectarian 'editing', but the Christian historian argues that these reported claims were in fact historically made. Since to the non-converted Jew any idea of man-worship was blasphemous, this Christian worship of Jesus was incredibly revolutionary and original. Unlike the age-old Jewish worship of a God whom 'no man hath seen', unlike even the cults of the pagan *goyim*, it was offered to a person who had been seen and heard as a human being, a god risen out of the common humanity of Galilee.

The Christian liturgy was the school where new converts learned about Jesus. There was obviously a difference between the Jesus of history and their Jesus of ritual experience. Cult personality is not the same thing as biographical personality. There have been in religious tradition instances of cult personality with little or no biographical basis. The cult personality comes to life in popular memory, which is not the same as historical memory; one does not seek photographic accuracy in a church ikon. In Christian worship the earthly life of Jesus was ritualized into liturgical drama, a fact which explains much of the difficulty the primitive documents present to historical enquiry. Though one may feel confident about certain main themes in the preaching of Jesus it is impossible to state how accurately his spoken words are preserved by the early cult and its documents. As time passes cult can elaborate its own modes of expression and develop whole styles of art in a life of its own. A Bach Passion, for instance, is to the listener a sublime human experience; but even though it is faithfully composed out of source narrative and out of traditional devotion it is a completely different experience from being an eye-witness on Golgotha when the rebel Jew was executed.[5]

The Jewish synagogue had been, as Philo reminds us, a 'house of instruction'. The Christian liturgy imitated this educative role. But its instruction was purely devotional; it was not rational *historia*, not the same kind of *paideia* as that furnished by the poems, speeches, histories and tragedies of Greek literature. Comparison of the various surviving forms of Christian worship brings into view a basic 'shape', which appears far more Jewish than Hellenic. The Greek convert from paganism must have missed in it the literary unity and aesthetic power of the great Athenian tragedies. Greek tragedy, developed out of the cult of Dionysos, is probably the most rational form of religious expression the world has yet known. But Semitic phraseology, the core of the Christian liturgy, did not build up rationality of form or the dramatic punctuation of 'beginning, middle and end'. Instead it followed the irregular contours of life and conversation, and its daily sequence came to be determined by the dates on which Christian saints happened to die. Its idiom was 'words of life' rather than words of reason. This Semitic idiom was repugnant to the Hellenic ear, and it seems too that the oriental cult of a crucified criminal was the object of popular contempt.[6] Hellenic repugnance to biblical idiom leaves its trace even on Christian minds. Augustine in his school days at Carthage thought the style of the scriptures barbaric; later in life he would not have turned back to them but for the influence of Saint Ambrose. Even when he was on the threshold of conversion and Ambrose advised him to read Isaiah he found 'the Lord's rhetoric' too much for him; he had already, however, been eagerly reading Saint Paul, for the ascetic directions he found in 'the book of the Apostle' were close to the spirituality of the Platonists (*Confessions* 7. 21; 9. 5).

Ancient philosophy was wedded to a literary style, supremely exemplified by Plato, alongside which the Semitic type of expression seemed barbarous. Antiquity had fostered dramatic beauty of dialogue and had also developed a scientific prose, both of which were foreign to the idiom of the scriptures. It is true that when we come to the fourth century, Christian writers like Gregory of Nazianzus and John Chrysostom can emulate the pagan stylists. But their studied imitation of the Attic writers is an admission of victory for the pagan intellect in this respect. Their philosophic style meant the adoption of a lot of the images and examples of myth and poetry stored in the magazine of pagan philosophy. For though philosophy is essentially abstract, cutting into concepts the concrete togetherness of reality, and pursuing an 'ancient feud' against poetry, it cannot entirely dispense with the language of sense. The imagery admitted into Greek philosophy and borrowed by Christianity was often distinctly pagan and alien to the original idiom of the faith.

The thought world of Judaism with its Oriental apocalyptic, ritual, blood sacrifice, and tortuous legislation, was foreign to the Greek philosophic mind. This tension between 'Jew and Greek' was deep-rooted and has remained in the European tradition: in any community of Europeans you are likely to discern the Socratic type and the Pauline type. The thoughts nourished by the early Christian meetings, even though spoken in Greek, were not Socratic, not informed by critical history, not opened by dialectic; they were time-based and place-bound within Judaism and could not claim the universality of philosophy.

Christian faith, nevertheless, possessed a motivation and persuasion unknown to philosophy. This sprang from intense devotion to the person of Jesus. We can sense it in extant phrases that were read in the Christian meetings; Jesus is the 'anointed one' (*christos*) of ancient Jewish hope; he is 'son of God'; he has spoken with the authority of JHWH; he has even risen from the dead and will appear again in splendour, inaugurating a new order. This was the idea of him which the faithful carried from their meetings. Though physical encounter with him was no longer possible the believers were not troubled: they were inspired by the image produced by liturgical devotion. This devotion was very different from the scientific satisfaction of contemplating the ordered motions of the stars or the immortal harmonies of geometry or the imitation of such harmony in human society. Christian devotion rested on the ritualized record of a person who had lived in a remote area of the Roman Empire, who proclaimed the nearness of a divine intervention in the life of Israel, of decisive importance to all other nations as well. The proclamation was not a matter for intellect, hardly even for writing. Rather it was a religious demand set before followers: the kingdom is at hand. Even when this 'good news' had been elaborated into liturgy it was still unlike anything philosophic; its main interest was the expectation of the second appearance of Jesus in divine glory to establish his 'Kingdom of God'. The lack of philosophic content becomes more evident still when one remembers that the audience of Jesus did not come from the educated class of Jews. An interesting perspective here is presented by the oppressed Jews of eastern Europe in the eighteenth century for whom the preaching of the Hasidic masters, based on miracle story and simple maxim, a prophetic idiom very like that of Jesus, provided spiritual consolation not available from the upper-class 'doctors of the law'. This is far from being a 'consolation of philosophy' deriving from cogency of idea. It is the appeal of a person.

Devotion produced ascetic discipline, and with a capacity for disciplined organization the Church impinged on the politics of the Empire with an impetus unknown to philosophy. The regular meetings established, and, as Pliny remarks, cemented by oath (*sacramento*) a familiar solidarity and an absolute refusal to share in any gesture of emperor-worship. Such obstinate standing apart from the universal empire in a 'hatred of the human race' irritated the authorities and prompted a long series of purges, from the persecution under Nero occasioned by the fire of Rome in A.D. 64 to the last and greatest offensive by Diocletian in 303.[7]

We have stressed the enormous difference separating the idiom of Jesus, and even that of the Hellenist early Church, from Greek philosophy. Yet, in the wake of persecution these incompatibles, philosophy and faith, were to meet. The religion which gained the harsh attention of the emperors began to attract the notice of philosophers towards the middle of the second century. Crescens the Cynic, followed the imperial attitude and, no doubt appealing to a general hatred of Christians in his popular audience, lectured against Christianity in Rome. Fronto, the tutor of Marcus Aurelius, condemned it as superstitious. Finally Celsus wrote (178–180) his long and closely reasoned criticism of it.

But educated believers had already entered the Christian ranks and these replied by making appeal to the authorities in cultured language. As a patristic group they are called the Apologists.[8] Quadratus, a philosopher from Asia, wrote an appealing defence to the Emperor Hadrian – though all we have of it is a rather unphilosophic paragraph recounting Christian miracles. Aristeides, from the home of philosophy, Athens, sent a treatise to the Emperor Antoninus (about A.D. 147) and a little later the same emperor and his sons were to read an Apologia from a travelling lecturer, Justin of Neapolis, who wore the short cloak of the Greek philosopher. Justin did not hesitate to connect Jesus with Socrates, to quote the Stoics about the end of the world, and to describe Christians as 'pious men and philosophers'. The reader approaches his work eager to note how a mind like his, inheriting the long tradition of Greek rationalism, reacted to the new oriental faith and especially to its ritual. The surprise is that though he has read so much pagan philosophy his attitude to it is hostile and alien. His lack of philosophic acumen is a disappointment. One is upset to meet his naïve assertion that Greek philosophy was plagiarized from the Jewish revelation; in this of course he was only voicing a view shared by other Christian, Jewish, and indeed pagan writers.

The Apologists, though of the literary social circles, resembled the Cynic preachers in their attempt to win the confidence of the lower classes. They felt that their new religious persuasion was of wider social relevance than their inherited culture. They realized too that rational philosophy was the one item of pagan culture which they could take as their ally in opposing the popular mythology and cults of paganism. Philosophy appeared to be the best means for the Jewish-born faith to contact its pagan environment, as even Paul on the Areopagus seemed to realize.

But the attempt to annex philosophy brought crisis. The philosophers who were converted to Christianity were no longer humanist rationalists like the pre-Socratic Xenophanes or the Sophists. Their interests were very syncretist. On their conversion many of them retained current preoccupation with the religious concept of 'salvation', mingled with a host of similar concepts from the Oriental mystery religions. Salvation was to be achieved by perfect knowledge (*gnosis*). They insisted that there were hidden truths in the scriptures which only the true Gnostic could discern. Gnosticism, however exotic its forms, had one genuinely Greek trait: it presented holiness as a matter of the intellect. But *Gnosis* was not a philosophic quest. It was a longing for mystical, intuitive, immediate, satisfaction of mind. It had the power of lulling the understanding and overcoming doubt. Its popular appeal was reflected in a profusion of sects, following diverse leaders: Simon Magus, Menander, Corinthus, Satornil, Basilides, Carpocras, Valentinus, Heracleon, Ptolemy, Marcus, and the greatest of all, Marcion, whose failure marks the end of the Gnostic crisis at the close of the second century.

The Gnostic movement is paralleled in the Hermetic literature, portions of which survive from the second century. This literature is a *pot-pourri* of religious notions characteristic of the age: astrology and occult science, esoteric doctrines of the soul and the 'unknown god' of the cosmos. Philosophic notions are mixed with the rest of this irrationalism, mainly ideas about Platonic emanation through subordinated hypostases, with names such as *Father, Mind, Word, Wisdom*. The Gnostic concept of ideal perfection (*pleroma*) appears in the Pauline epistles. Gnostic sects tended to be exclusive elites each apparently well organized, but lacking over-all federation.

The Catholic reaction came in the form of developed organization. The ecclesiastical official took the place of the spontaneous prophet and the visionary teacher. Prophecy where it continued was strictly supervised. Church administration brought into prominence the priest-bishops (*episkopoi, sacerdotes*), each with his team of assistants. Christian organization had behind it the example of the Jewish communities of the Diaspora, each united in itself and yet closely attached to the spiritual centre of Jerusalem. And so Christianity which had begun as a great surge of Jewish Messianic hope, and now risked division into countless philosophic sects, came to have the stability and definition of organized authority. Adherence to tradition was preached, the canon of biblical books was determined, a formal creed took clear shape, the office of bishop was accorded authoritative status. Prophecy revived for a few brief years (*c.* 160–170) in the person of Montanus and his enthusiasts, who urged a vigorous moral asceticism in place of Gnostic metaphysics. But their over-strict asceticism would have limited the human appeal of the Church, and episcopal foresight and authority soon checked their extremes of thought and practice. Thereafter the Church had definite institution and government, achieving a solidarity and a confidence of victory which the philosophers had not been able to arouse. The philosophers in their liberal debates had never thought of a universal teamwork of this sort, nor of enforcing any of their tenets universally. Here Christians had learnt more perhaps from Roman imperialism than from Greek dialectic. The Latin Church has never erred far from the attitude of Cato, the typical Roman in Cicero's dialogue: 'When it comes to religion I follow the *pontifex maximus* and not Zeno or Cleanthes or Chrysippus' (*de nat. deor.* 3. 2). The figure of the Church which appeared in one of the visions of Hermas (second century) displayed a more imperious authority than the Lady Philosophy who appeared to console the Neoplatonist. We have now passed from the history of idea to the history of institution.

Organization checked the vagaries of prophecy, and it encouraged the development of an official theology. The cradle of theological speculation was Alexandria, a city which had been founded in the wake of Alexander's conquest of the East, and then, with its magnificent library, built by Alexander's Egyptian successors, the Hellenized Ptolemys, gradually took from Athens the intellectual leadership of the Greek world. The Jewish community there had become so strongly Hellenized that, in the reign of Ptolemy Philadelphus (285–246 B.C.), the Septuagint Greek translation of the Bible was made for the synagogue readings. We have already noted how Philo carried Jewish Hellenism a stage further by attempting a synthesis between the Bible and pagan philosophy. The Alexandrian master, Ammonius Saccas, regarded as the founder of Neoplatonism, though he wrote nothing, may have taken ideas from Philo, may indeed for a time have been a Christian. Plotinus was his pupil, though it was in Rome that Plotinus founded his own school in A.D. 244. The religious emphasis of Plotinus's thought made it congenial for Christian study. He was acquainted with Gnosticism, but criticized it as alien to true Platonism. He is a remarkable phenomenon in the history of Greek thought, a mystic using the apparatus of philosophy as method of expression for his ethical ideal of intuitive identity with 'the One', the transcendent unity of reality. The religious rather than the philosophic elements of his thought caught the attention of a large school of followers led by men like Porphyry, Iamblichus, Proclus. For them philosophy was a form of holiness. Neoplatonism was to have a profound effect on Christian theological tradition. Latin traces of this appear in the scriptural commentaries of Saint Ambrose, and it was a reading of Plotinus translated into Latin which set Augustine's thoughts in the direction of Christianity. The mystic and ascetic implications of Plotinus's work were embodied in the writings of the monk known as Dionysius the pseudo-Areopagite, and so entered the tradition of monasticism. Because of its rich synthesis of previous thought Neoplatonism was in the Late Empire the strongest pagan alternative to Christianity. But it lacked popular appeal and like all the philosophies it lacked hierarchical organization.

Clement and his pupil, Origen, of Alexandria, taking over from Philo the effort to unite philosophy and revelation, are the foundation stones of Christian theology.[9] Origen was a friend of Plotinus, a Platonist, and in a sense a Gnostic. For him, as for Gregory of Nyssa after him, 'knowledge of reality' (*gnōsis tōn ontōn*) is the supreme end. Clement, his predecessor in the catechetical school of Alexandria, had also described the act of assent involved in faith to be an inner gnosis. It was such hazardous attempts to intellectualize the non-intellectual data of religion which brought Christian theology into being. But theology remained subject to the vigilance of episcopal organization, and it is significant that the brilliant Origen himself was to lose prestige through ecclesiastical disapproval. Heresy was now as suspect as prophecy had formerly been.

Political structure seems to have been in the Church from the very beginning. The organization seems to have passed from a democratic to a monarchic principle, and with this there developed a distinction between clergy and laity, and the clergy rose eventually to a social eminence which enhanced their command. The capacity of the organization to remain united over the whole extent of the empire seems the strongest factor in its victory. The cults of the Empire had been local and various: only emperor-worship, Rome-worship, was universal. It is remarkable how the Christian groups, so separated over a large area, kept their thoughts, sentiments, enthusiasms in a single unity. There was constant exchange of letters, making full use of the imperial communication system; there were meetings of bishops in synod; there were the doctrinal treatises devoted to unity; there was the central prestige of the Roman bishop. The unity thus achieved appears remarkable. It remains so even when we have taken into account the notable incidence of schism and heresy. Heresy was declared to be a diabolical first-fruit of pagan philosophy. But the real threat of heresy, which at times was local or nationalist, was to the political structure of the Church. Later, in the converted Empire, it was also a threat to the state; which explains the fervour of the converted Emperors in eradicating it in favour of the new universal religion which they adopted as a force of political cohesion.[10]

All imperial attacks on the *religio illicita* were unequal in the end to Christian obstinacy and organization, and Constantine was shrewd enough to see that here was a religion to have on the side of Empire and not against it. He therefore, in the year 312, professed allegiance to the persecuted faith. From then the Christian attitude to Emperor and Empire changed from curse to blessing. The triumph of the persecuted proletarian movement was soon complete, a model, indeed, to any subsequent revolutionary:

> It is now, almost to the year, sixteen hundred years since a dangerous party of revolt made a great commotion in the Roman Empire. It undermined religion and all the foundations of the state; it flatly denied that Caesar's will was the supreme law; it was without a fatherland, international; it spread over all countries of the Empire from Gaul to Asia, and beyond the frontiers of the Empire. It had

long carried on an underground agitation in secret; for a considerable time, however, it had felt itself strong enough to come out into the open. This party of revolt, who were known by the name of Christians, was also strongly represented in the army; whole legions were Christian. When they were ordered to attend the sacrificial ceremonies of the pagan established church, in order to do the honours there, the soldier-rebels had the audacity to stick popular emblems – crosses – on their helmets in protest. Even the wonted barrack cruelties of their superior officers were fruitless. The Emperor Diocletian could no longer quietly look on while order, obedience and discipline in his army were being undermined. He intervened energetically, while there was still time. He passed an anti-Socialist, I should say anti-Christian, law. The meetings of the rebels were forbidden, their meeting halls were closed or even pulled down, the Christian badges, crosses, etc., were, like the red handkerchiefs in Saxony, prohibited. Christians were declared incapable of holding offices in the state, they were not to be allowed even to become corporals. Since there were not available at that time judges so well trained in 'respect of persons' as Herr von Köller's anti-revolt bill assumes, the Christians were forbidden out of hand to seek justice before a court. This exceptional law was also without effect. The Christians tore it down from the walls with scorn; they are even supposed to have burnt the Emperor's palace in Nicomedia over his head. Then the latter revenged himself by the great persecution of Christians in the year 303, according to our chronology. It was the last of its kind. And it was so effective that seventeen years later the army consisted overwhelmingly of Christians, and the succeeding autocrat of the whole Roman Empire, Constantine, called the Great by the priests, proclaimed Christianity as the State religion!

F. ENGELS, *Introduction* to KARL MARX, *The Class Struggles in France, 1848–50,* (London 1895), trans. Lawrence, London, 1934

The lack of comparable organization in the pagan opposition was painfully felt by the Emperor Julian who attempted a return to paganism. His brief reign (A.D. 361–3) was devoted to a desperate attempt to make the current Neoplatonism into a church, modelled on the Christian system of episcopal government and organized charity. He forbade Christians to occupy teaching posts, ordering them back into their churches to expound 'the barbarities of Matthew and Luke'. But the Greek philosophic religion (*Hellenismos*) he was trying to establish was far from having the full quality and appeal of Greek rationalism, for Hellenic thought had now begun to suffer what Gilbert Murray (borrowing the phrase from Bury, though it had been used by Rohde) called 'a failure of nerve'. The Christian organization proved superior to Julian's Hellenism. The long struggle with Gnosticism and Neo-platonism had assured the Church that philosophy could not defeat an efficient political system. Besides, Christianity possessed a social dyna-mism unknown to Greek philosophy. It had inflexible zeal, hope of after-life to compensate for present hardship, confidence in miracle, strict morality, and it was a society that rapidly made itself universal within the universal Roman state. It possessed a common way of life, a common social security in face of danger, and it gave those who were underprivileged in the large anonymous society of the Empire a sense of belonging.[11]

There had been a continual menace of persecution during the second century, the century of Gnosticism. The fact that the communities were often dispersed by force increased the risk of doctrinal disunity. They hid within their walls; even their architecture does not show its face in the open air like the pagan shrines. The third century, that of Clement and Origen, was more tranquil. But in the fourth century when the Emperor was converted the Church could begin in earnest her 'despoiling of the Egyptians', assimilating the pagan philosophy to promote her own designs.

At times the pagans regarded the growth of the Church with indif-ference or tolerance. Christian influence even makes its mark here and there in the pagan authors: in Philostratus and Numenius, in the Neo-platonists, in the schools of Athens and Alexandria, in Themistius, Julian and Porphyry, in Libanius's attitude to his pupil, John Chrysostom. But the pagans eventually become more hostile and isolated, realizing the size of the social change which had occurred. They came to see that their political forms and culture had become incapsulated in the Chris-tian religion.

The Christian assimilation of philosophy was part of a much larger syncretism. The victorious religion assimilated cultural forms, modes of education, religious rituals, political methods, pagan institutions. Gradually there occurred a sort of secularization in the structure of the Church society. For instance, the taxation unit (*dioikesis*) of the Empire was made the unit of Church administration. *Romanus* and *Christianus* soon became synonymous. The procedure of the pagan senate was imitated in the bishops' synod. The itinerant sophist gave place to the preacher. The farm techniques of Cato and Varro were adopted by the self-sufficient monastery farm, and the quadrangular country house set the model of the monastic building. The prerogatives of the *pontifex maximus* fell to the bishop of Rome. The rubrics of the pagan religious calendars (*fasti*) now regulated the canonical hours of the Divine Office. The philosopher's *pallium* clothed monk or apologist. Literary culture served study of the Bible. The Emperor submitted to the bishop, or else claimed episcopal status for himself. Philosophy was only one part of this larger synthesis. The whole secular culture and polity thus subsumed into the Church eventually laid the political foundation of medieval Europe, so that a modern apologist can declare that 'the Faith is Europe and Europe is the Faith'. In this religious–political amalgam the historian will according to his special interest encounter a variety of non-Christian elements: Oriental ideas of a divine *kosmokrator*, traces of Greek gods and heroes, cults of the dead and fertility cults, themes of mystery initiation. Indeed the historian will have difficulty in setting himself sympathetically within the manifestations of European Christianity unless he nourishes in his soul some feeling for the pagan gods. In the converted Empire he finds some Christians whose mentality is hardly distinguishable from that of the pagans, and who regard pagan philosophy as a thing of 'holiness'. Conversion of the Empire involved a certain conversion of the Church towards paganism.[12]

Strange though all this metamorphosis may seem, the indications of all the evidence suggest that Christianity was an organic development. The first creative impulse had come in response to a Jewish prophet urging preparedness for the imminent appearance of the 'Kingdom of God' in Israel. His following appears in our earliest evidence as a band of close-knit communities whose language is no longer of Israel but of the Empire. This group is disciplined and intensely devout in its cult of the founder as divine. Its mode of expression is only superficially Greek, for it is alien to pagan culture and has no truck with gentile 'wisdom'. The community, though proletarian, possesses a social dynamism that impinges on the upper-class imperial bureaucracy and evokes persecution. Its pertinacity, however, and its strict morality attract upper-class converts and some of these write philosophic defences of their new faith. Philosophic thought thus enters the Church and threatens it with liberal diversity of doctrines, for the rationalist method of philosophy, though useful in attacking mythology, is apt to dilute belief, and a spiritualizing tendency in current thought means risk of absorption in polytheistic paganism. But this challenge only

An unpublished fragment of the Fourth Gospel (Pap. Rylands Gr. 457, c. A.D. 120.

Reproduced by permission of the John Rylands Library, Manchester

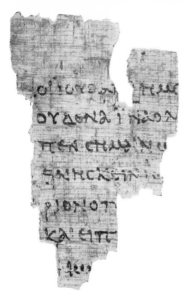

Recto   Verso

The Jews said: *We are not allowed to execute anybody. This fulfilled the statement of Jesus indicating the kind of death which awaited him. Pilate went into the praetorium again and called Jesus and said to him: Are you the resistance-leader of the Jews? . . .*

. . . For this I was born; for this I came into the world, to be witness to the truth. Everyone who lives out of the truth listens to my words. Pilate asked him: What does 'truth' mean? As he said this he went out again to the Jews and told them: I find no cause for condemnation . . .

(Pap. Rylands Gr. 457)

elicits still firmer organization and the growth of an official theology. Then comes the conversion of the pagan elite, and their culture is assimilated. When this happens the community is certainly far away from its beginnings in Judaism. But still the *élan* inspiring the development seems continuous with that communal momentum first evoked in unphilosophic peasants by a Jewish teacher whose every remembered word or gesture was uniquely endowed with heroic appeal.

DOCUMENTARY NOTES

I

For a basic biographical document about Jesus we can turn to an outside witness, the Roman historian Tacitus who, writing about A.D. 110, mentions the origin of Christianity in connection with his description of the burning of Rome in A.D. 64. His account shows how the early Christians in Rome, regarded as a sect of Jews, were unpopular with the Roman mob. But, more important, it records as a sober item of Roman history the one central, indubitable fact about Jesus – his execution.

No human resources, no lavish donations by Nero or expiatory offerings to the gods, would remove a damning suggestion that Rome had been burnt on the Emperor's orders. To scotch the rumour Nero invented culprits. He punished with the most elaborate torture people whom the mob hated for their abominable practices and called Christians. The founder of the sect, Christus, had been executed in the reign of Tiberius by the procurator Pontius Pilate. The degrading superstition was repressed for the time being, but it broke out again, not only in Judaea, where the mischief had begun, but even in districts of Rome itself – where sordid and shameful activities from all quarters meet and coalesce. At first those Christians who admitted their belief were arrested, and then on the information they furnished an enormous number of others were condemned, not so much for being guilty of the fire as for hatred of the human race. Their death was made into a spectacle of entertainment. Some were dressed in animal skins and devoured by dogs. Others were fixed to crosses, and when night fell some were set alight as torches. Nero had given over his gardens for the occasion and put on circus games. He himself mixed with the crowd, dressed up as a chariot-rider, or rode about in his car. Although these

Christians were guilty and deserved the severest punishment, they now excited pity, for their sacrifice seemed not so much to serve the public interest as the cruelty of one man.

TACITUS, *Annals* 15. 44

2

In the Christian evidence we find some remarkably early manuscript fragments of 'Gospels'. The earliest of these is a fragment of the canonical fourth Gospel. It comes from the account of the trial of Jesus, and is a little cameo of the difference between Jewish and Hellenic attitudes to the word 'truth'. A number of other fragments have come to light from Oxyrhynchus and elsewhere; these are now known, because of the discovery of a complete Coptic translation, to belong to the Gnostic 'Gospel of Thomas'. They are a collection of 'sayings' (logia) and, when we allow for the sectarian editing, give us an idea of the primitive sources out of which much of the four canonical gospels was constructed. The sayings are very much in keeping with the Jewish Rabbinical tradition.

The Jews said: 'We are not allowed to execute anybody.' This fulfilled the statement of Jesus indicating the kind of death which awaited him. Pilate went into the praetorium again and called Jesus and said to him: 'Are you the resistance-leader of the Jews?'

'. . . For this I was born; for this I came into the world, to be witness to the truth. Everyone who lives out of the truth listens to my words.' Pilate asked him: 'What does *truth* mean?' As he said this he went out again to the Jews and told them: 'I find no cause for condemnation . . .'

Pap. Rylands Gr. 457 (c. A.D. 120) (John 18: 31–8), ed. C. H. Roberts, An Unpublished Fragment of the Fourth Gospel in the John Rylands Library, Manchester, 1935

Jesus said to the lawyers: 'Punish every transgressor and lawbreaker and not me. . . .' Turning towards the rulers of the people he said this: 'Examine the Writings in which you think you possess life: it is they that bear witness to me. Do not think that I have come to accuse you to my Father, for Moses, in whom you have placed your hope, is already your accuser.' And when they said, 'We know that God spoke to Moses, but we do not know you or where you come from,' Jesus answered: 'Now your unbelief is under accusation. . . .'

. . . to drag him, and gathering stones together, to stone him. And the leaders laid hands on him to take him and give him over to the crowd. But they were not able to take him because the hour of his handing-over had not yet arrived. He (the Lord) escaped from their hands and went away.

And a leper came up to him and said: 'Rabbi Jesus, I was travelling along with lepers and eating with them in the inn, and I myself caught leprosy. Now if it is your will I shall be cleansed.' The Lord said to him: 'It is my will. Be cleansed.' All at once the leprosy left him. And the Lord told him: 'Start off and show yourself to the priests. . . .'

. . . They came to him and tested him with questions. 'Rabbi Jesus, we know that you have come from God, for the things you do bear better witness than all the prophets. So tell us: is it right to pay to kings what is claimed by their government? Should we pay or not?' Jesus, knowing their mind, said to them in anger: 'Why do you address me with the word Teacher on your lips, when you do not listen to what I say? Isaiah made a fitting prophecy about you when he said: "This people honours me with their lips but their heart is far away from me. It is empty reverence they pay me, teaching man-made dogmas and injunctions." . . .'

. . . Jesus as he walked along the bank of the river Jordan stood and stretched out his right hand . . . and sprinkled . . .

Papyrus Egerton 2 (c. A.D. 150), ed. H. I. BELL and T. C. SKEAT, *Fragments of an Unknown Gospel and other Early Christian Papyri*, British Museum, 1935

These are the words which Jesus the living Lord spoke and which Judas who is also called Thomas wrote. He said: 'Everyone who listens to these words will not taste death.'
Jesus says: 'He who seeks must not rest until he finds, and when he finds he will be astonished, and being astonished he will be king, and being king he will rest.'
Jesus says: 'If they who draw you say that the kingdom is in the sky, then the birds of the air are there before you; if they say that it is under the earth then the fishes of the sea are there before you. But the Kingdom of Heaven is both outside and within you, and he who

knows himself will find it. Know yourselves and you will be known, and you will know that you are sons of the living Father. But if you do not know yourselves you will be in poverty, and you are poverty.'

Jesus says: 'An old man will not hesitate to ask an infant of seven days about the place of life and he will live. For many of the first will be last and the last first, and they will be one only.'

Jesus says: 'What is not before your sight and is concealed from you will be revealed to you. There is nothing hidden which will not be made clear, nothing buried which will not be raised.'

His disciples question him: 'How shall we fast and how shall we pray and how shall we give arms and what observances shall we keep concerning food?'

Jesus says: 'Do not lie. And what you hate do not practise. Everything is clear to the truth.'

Gospel of Thomas 1–5. Pap. Oxyrhynchus 654, ed. P. P. GRENFELL and A. S. HUNT, *The Oxyrhynchus Papyri*, vol. 4, London, 1903

'. . . and then you will see how to take out the speck that is in the eye of your brother.'

Jesus says: 'If you do not fast as regards the world you will never find the Kingdom of God; and if you do not make a sabbath of the sabbath you will not see the Father.'

Jesus says: 'I stood in the middle of the world and was seen by them in the flesh, and I found them all drunken, and I found no one thirsting, and my soul is distressed over the sons of men, for they are blind in their heart and do not see. . . . poverty.'

Jesus says: 'Wherever there are two they are not without God, and wherever there is one alone, I say, I am with him. Raise up the stone and there you will find me; split the wood and I am there.'

Jesus says: 'A prophet is not acceptable in his fatherland, and a doctor does not perform cures on those who know him.'

Jesus says: 'A city built on top of a high hill and fortified can neither fall nor be hidden.'

Gospel of Thomas 27–33. Pap. Oxyrhynchus 1 (c. A.D. 250), ed. P. P. GRENFELL and A. S. HUNT, *The Oxyrhynchus Papyri*, vol. 1, London, 1898

'Do not worry from early morning until late evening nor from evening until morning about what food you will eat or what dress you will put on. You are far better than the lilies which grow without carding or spinning. Having one garment what more do you need? Who can add to your stature? He will give you your garment.' His disciples say to him: 'When will you be manifest to us and when shall we see you?' He says: 'When you are stripped and are not ashamed . . .' Jesus said: 'They took the key of knowledge and hid it. They did not enter themselves and they did not open to those who were entering.'

Gospel of Thomas 37–40. Pap. Oxyrhynchus 655 (third century), ed. P. P. GRENFELL and A. S. HUNT, *The Oxyrhynchus Papyri*, vol. 4, London, 1903

3

The Jewish scene in which the preaching of Jesus made its appearance had undergone Greek influence. There were synagogues built in Greek style where the Bible was read and explained in Greek. Parts of the Septuagint Bible had in fact been written by Hellenized Jews and show Hellenic influence. In the Wisdom books, for instance, we find mention of Plato's four cardinal virtues and the idea of Mind or Wisdom as an emanant entity distinct from God.

And if anyone loves Justice her labours are the virtues (*aretai*): for She teaches Temperance and Prudence, Justice and Fortitude, than which there is nothing better in life for men.

Septuagint: Wisdom of Solomon 8. 7

The Lord possessed me in the beginning of his ways, before he made anything from the beginning.

Wisdom is a vapour rising from the power of God, a pure emanation of the glory of the omnipotent God.

Septuagint: Proverbs 8. 22; Wisdom 7. 25

4

Paul, a product of Hellenistic Judaism, has some ideas in common with the Gnostic philosophers. He knows the Natural Law of the Stoics. He shows the first traces of a habit which was to gain ground in later Christian writers, of viewing Christianity in the light of the supreme cultural idea of the Greeks, that of Form: Christian faith is a process of intellectual formation (morphosis, paideia).

Being named a Jew . . . you are persuaded that you are a leader of the blind, a light in the dark, a corrector of the foolish, a teacher of the young, that you hold in the Law the formative power (*morphosis*) of knowledge (*gnosis*) and truth; teacher of your neighbour, why do you not teach yourself?

PAUL, *Letter to the Romans* 2. 20

Yet the keynote of Paul's writing is not the paideia *of Greek thought, but the worship of Jesus as* Christos. *This worship motivates and trains the Christian communities. Like the synagogue meetings the Christian gathering was meant to be a 'house of instruction'.*

5

The Apologist Justin gives a clearer picture of the liturgical meeting than the New Testament passages do.

On the day named after the sun all those who live in cities or in the country gather together and the memoirs of the Apostles or the writings of the prophets are read out as long as time permits. When the reader has finished the one who is in charge admonishes or exhorts us to follow the excellent examples presented by the reading. Then we all rise together and offer prayers, and then, as I have said, bread and wine and water are brought. Then the leader recites prayers and thanksgiving devoutly and the people assent to him by saying 'Amen'. Then each receives a share of the offerings over which thanksgiving has been pronounced, and through the deacons some is sent to those who are absent. People who have means make a contribution, each as he feels or thinks fit, and this collection is laid before him who presides so that he may help orphans, widows, those who are ill or impoverished, prisoners, or strangers staying with us: in a word, his task is to look after everyone in need.

JUSTIN, *First Apology* 67, (PG 6. 429)

A Roman caricature of the second century ridicules Christian worship. It shows a worshipper standing before a crucified figure with an ass's head and has a roughly scrawled Greek caption: *Alexamenos worships his god*

ΑΛΕΞΑΜΕΝΟC CΕΒΕΤΕ ΘΕΟΝ

R. LANCIANI, *Ancient Rome in the Light of Recent Excavations*, Riverside Press, Boston and New York, 1892, p. 122 (Alinan photograph)

6

The un–Hellenic character of early Christian faith was mocked by the pagans at the popular as well as the philosophic level. A Roman caricature of the second century ridicules Christian worship. It shows a worshipper standing before a crucified figure with an ass's head, and has a roughly scrawled Greek caption: 'Alexamenos worships his god' (Alexamenos sebetai theon).

Educated pagans criticized the fanatic and illiberal obstinacy of the Christian believers. Also, their Semitic style of thought and expression seemed detestable. Yet the advance of the religion in spite of imperial ban puzzled the philosophers.

What a fine soul it is that is ever prepared for its destiny, whether this is to be liberated from the body, or to be totally extinguished, or to be dissolved into its elements, or to remain a unity! This preparedness should come from personal decision and not from mere partisanship (like the Christians); it should come rationally and nobly and in a manner likely to influence others, not just in the manner of a tragic actor.

MARCUS AURELIUS, *To Himself* 11. 3. 2

You might as well try to convert followers of Moses or followers of Christ as these doctors who are devotees of philosophic sects.

GALEN, *On the Pulse* 3. 3. (*Corpus Medic. Graec.* 8. 657)

. . . one should not from the very beginning learn about laws that have no rational demonstration, and in matters where they are least necessary, as happens when one joins the school of Moses and Christ.

GALEN, *On the Pulse* 2. 4 (*Corpus Medic. Graec.* 8. 579)

7

Records of the persecution trials strike a modern note in their totalitarian thoroughness. The state machinery seems at first sight invincible with its ubiquitous bureaucracy of local commissions and 'certificates of loyalty'. On the other hand, the Christians seem to have inherited into their faith some-

thing of the self-sacrificing resistance with which the Jews had defended the rock of Masada.

The proconsul Saturninus read out the decree from the tablet: 'Because Speratus, Nartzalus, Cittinus, Donata, Vestia, Secunda, and the others who have admitted that they live according to Christian rite, have obstinately continued to do so when they were given the opportunity to return to Roman practice, it is my decision that they be punished by the sword.'
Speratus said, 'We offer thanks to God.'
Nartzalus said, 'We are in heaven as martyrs today; thanks be to God.'

Acts of the Martyrs of Scillium (Carthage, A.D. 180), ed. R. Knopf, Tubingen, 1929

Aurelia Bellias . . . and her daughter Kapinis to those in charge of the sacrifices in the village of Theadelphia:

We have always made sacrifice to the gods and now in your presence and following your instructions I have poured a libation and made sacrifice and tasted the sacred offerings. I therefore request you to sign this for us.

We, Aurelius Serenus and Aurelius Hermas, saw you sacrificing.
Signed by me: HERMAS.

First year of the Emperor Decius. . . . Pauni 27 (21 June, A.D. 250).

Papyrus Michigan 158 (Egypt, A.D. 250), ed. J. G. Winter, *Univ. of Michigan Studies, Humanistic Series* 40 (1936), p. 134

8

The Apologists venture into Greek philosophic territory and speak its language.

Yet under these Emperors the truth again produced many defenders who fought against the godless opinions not only by oral attack but also by written demonstrations. . . . In the time of the Emperor Hadrian, Justin, a genuine lover of true philosophy, was still occupied in practising the studies of the Greeks. . . . In his book (*Apology* 2. 12) he shows that his conversion from Greek philosophy to the worship

of God did not happen irrationally but came about by rational judgement. This is what he says: 'At the time when I was elated by the doctrines of Plato I witnessed attacks on the Christians. But I noticed that
they were fearless in the face of death and of everything men consider
terrible. And I reflected that it was absurd to imagine that their lives
were given to evil and pleasure-seeking . . .'

EUSEBIUS, Church History 4. 7. 15 (PG 20. 315 ff.)

I pray and strive to be seen as a Christian not just because the teachings
of Plato are alien to those of Christ. Plato's views are not similar in all
respects to Christian teaching, any more than are statements of the
Stoics, of the poets, of the historians. Each of these people spoke
truth in proportion to the innate share he had in the divine seminal
reason (logos spermatikos). . . . Whatever has been truthfully said by any
human being belongs to us Christians.

JUSTIN, Apology 2. 13. 2 (PG 6. 465)

9

*In the wake of philosophic apologetics comes the full impact of philosophy,
so evident in the work of the great third-century Alexandrians, Clement and
Origen, and in the fourth-century Cappadocian Fathers.*

What I have written may suffice to show . . . Origen's proficiency in
the Greek disciplines. He defends himself against certain of his detractors
who criticized his study of such matters, in one of his letters, as follows:
'When I devoted myself to the Word and news got about of my interests I was visited sometimes by heretics, sometimes by students of
Greek subjects, especially philosophers. So I decided to examine the
doctrines of the heretics and also whatever the philosophers professed
concerning truth. In doing this I was only imitating my predecessor
Pantainos, the benefactor of so many people, who was quite well
grounded in these studies. I was also copying Heraklas who now holds
a seat in the presbytery at Alexandria; I came upon him when he was
attending a teacher of the philosophic disciplines, who had had him
already as a pupil for five years before I began to attend such lectures.
Heraklas, who previously had worn ordinary clothing, now under
the influence of his teacher changed into the robe of a philosopher. He

wears it to this day and he never tires of studying Greek books with all his might.' That is what Origen said in defence of his Greek training.

EUSEBIUS, *Church History* 6. 19. 11 (*PG* 20. 567)

Eunomius . . . hales Basil into court on the charge that his language follows the philosophy of the pagan outsiders; that he sets limits to God's providence by saying that names were not put on things originally by God himself but by man; that Basil is fighting in the ranks of the atheists, taking up arms against providence and admiring pagan doctrines rather than the laws of God.

GREGORY of Nyssa, *Against Eunomius's second book* (*PG* 45. 909 ff.)

10

The unified organization of the Church, so different from the disagreeing sects of philosophers, at once gave confidence to its members and outlawed extravagant initiative among them.

The Church having received this belief preached by the Apostles carefully preserves it, and though she is dispersed throughout the world she preserves it as if she lived in one house. She believes the same doctrines everywhere, as if she had a single heart and soul, and she teaches them harmoniously everywhere as if she had but one tongue. The languages of the world may be different, but the message handed on by the Church is one and the same.

IRENAEUS, *Against Heresies* 1. 10. 2 (*PG* 7. 552)

11

The rival effort of paganism to create a philosophic 'church' based on Platonic doctrines is illustrated in the writings of Julian.

To Arsakios, High-Priest of Galatia:
   Hellenism, our religion, is not yet making the progress expected of it. This is the fault of us who profess it. The rites of our gods are grand and glittering, surpassing all desire and hope. May Nemesis be kind if I declare that more progress has been made in a short time than

anyone could have dared to pray for a little time ago. But why are we satisfied with this much? Do we not see clearly that the atheism of the Christians has progressed, simply because of their hospitality to strangers, care for the tombs of the dead, and a show of holiness? All of these things we must attend to. It is not just you alone who must do so but all the priests of Galatia without exception. You must importune or persuade them into the right attitude. Remove them from their priestly duties, if they, along with their wives, children and servants, stay away from divine service, content to live with domestics or children or wives who show no honour to the gods and prefer atheism to worship. Exhort your priests not to go to theatres, not to drink in taverns, not to conduct any base unbecoming art or trade. Honour those who obey you, expel those who disobey. Set up several houses of hospitality in each city of your area, so that strangers may have the benefit of our generosity, shown not just to our own people but to any outsiders who need it. I have already made provision for the supplies you will need. I have ordered three thousand measures of corn to be assigned for all Galatia, and six thousand bottles of wine. A fifth of this is to be spent on the poor who wait upon the priests, and the rest must be distributed to strangers and those who request it. It is a crying shame that our people are left without our service, whereas among the Jews nobody ever has to beg, and the impious followers of the Galilean are able to care for some of our poor as well as their own. Teach the members of our Hellenist religion to contribute to public charity, and make the Hellenist villagers dedicate their first fruits to the service of religion. Get our Greek people accustomed to this doing of good, telling them that it is an age-old tradition of theirs, as Homer reminds us. . . . If I hear that you are successfully carrying out this programme it will give me very great pleasure indeed.

Visit state officials at their homes only very rarely; instead contact them by letter. When one of them enters a city no priest should go outside to receive him; but whenever he visits a temple the priest should meet him within the porch. The official as he enters should not be preceded by a military guard, and the people should follow as they please. For, the moment he steps into the precinct he is a private citizen; you know that the ruler of all that goes on inside the temple is yourself. This is the divine law and those who sincerely obey it are good, while those who resist it are ambitious and vain.

JULIAN, *Letter* 49, ed. F. C. Hertlein, Teubner, 1875, p. 552

12

*In the Empire we come upon some Christian minds decidedly more philo-
sophic than devotional, who still believed, as the pagan tradition from Plato
to Cicero had believed, that philosophy is ultimate. Christians were bound
to be affected by the tendency of Greek intellectuals to convert their religious
aspirations into the effort of thought and scholarship. Mental culture, not faith,
came to be regarded by the Greek mind as the ultimate value. Menander's
line, 'Of all human things the greatest is* paideia', *would have been perfectly
acceptable to Hellenists of the Christian Empire such as Synesius the bishop
or Boethius the senator.*

My previous letter meant to show that philosophy should be chosen in
preference to your profession of the forum. . . . You pass for a patriotic
man, but I would claim to be the same. You practise oratory, and I
admit your criticism that I do not, except perhaps that correct and noble
kind which I do not feel even Plato tries to describe. But I esteem
philosophy and prefer it to all human goods. But what does philosophy
contribute to the city? It suggests modes of living which are worthy of
rational intention.

SYNESIUS of Cyrene, *Letter to Pylaimenes (PG* 66. 1473)

But you, Philosophy, dwelling within me, drove all desire of mortal
things from the home of my soul, and under your eyes there could be
no occasion for sacrilege. Day after day you instilled in my ears and
thoughts that saying of Pythagoras, 'Follow God'. It was not in character that the protection of evil spirits should ever be sought by me,
the man whom you had chosen for the ideal of making him 'like to
God'. I am also defended from all shadow of such guilt by the innocent
sanctuary of my home, by the company of upright friends, and by my
father-in-law, Symmachus, who is a saintly man and as worthy of
reverence as you, Philosophy, yourself.

BOETHIUS, *The Consolation of Philosophy* I. 4. 38

IV

The Synthesis of Faith and Rational Philosophy

The assimilation of pagan thought meant that Christian vocabulary became thoroughly philosophic. *Dogma* the Greek word for philosophic tenet, is now used to denote the teaching of Christ. There is a wedding of Semitic and Hellenic, Plato read from one hand and the Bible from the other. The 'wisdom of God' meets the 'wisdom of the world', the inspired authority of scriptural revelation meets dialectical enquiry. But this does not mean that after New Testament times Christianity became a philosophy in the ancient sense. The big difference between Christian philosophic prose and pagan is that the former is laced throughout with borrowings from the Scripture.

There was no shortage of problems to which philosophic enquiry might be applied: the relationship between faith and reason; the relationship between the persons of the Trinity and the philosopher's Logos or Forms; the relationship between the human Christ and the divine Trinity; amid all this multiplicity, the preservation of monotheism. Philosophy was bound by its eristic nature to result in variety of answer, and for the new religion such variety engendered heresies. Controversy over these was the prime factor in the development of Church doctrine.

In face of heresy the urge of the Church was to define and formulate. The Church Fathers therefore are philosophic almost in spite of themselves. Cyril of Jerusalem, for example, is no friend of philosophy – he calls the philosophers 'gentiles' (*Hellenes*) – but yet he cannot quite avoid using their terminology.

Philosophic notions worked their way through each successive group of Greek patristic writers: first, the Apologists; then the Alexandrians, Clement and Origen; then the great fourth-century Cappadocians, Gregory of Nyssa, Gregory of Nazianzus and Basil; the Antiochene, John Chrysostom; the writers of the Late Empire, Dionysius, Maximus,

Nemesius, Aeneas of Gaza, Philoponus; finally John Damascene and the medieval Greek schoolmen.

All the disciplines of pagan 'wisdom' were admitted within the gates. Logic brought in the urge to define, to distinguish and to demonstrate belief by syllogism; it also contributed categories, like those of substance and accident, of quantity, quality and relation, the notions of being and non-being, potency and act, matter and form. Ancient metaphysics and physics served the doctrine of divine providence and creation; here also were enlisted the *logos* and the Platonic transcendental forms of goodness, unity, truth, beauty, being. From the ancient cosmologies came theories of matter and form and movement, and from the psychologies intellect and will. Ethical writings provided the pervasive notion of natural law, theories of finality and social utopias.

Perhaps one can best illustrate the ferment produced by the mingling of these diverse forces, religion and philosophy, by taking dominant headings of pagan philosophy and exemplifying some details of their reincarnation in Christian thought, limiting our view, for convenience, to the Greek tradition.

One thinks of beginning with the concept of knowledge, for this is bound to be influenced by the impact of faith.[1] The objective reference of truth, reality, will also very likely be modified.[2] Then there is the supreme reality, God, about whom both philosophy and faith make pronouncements.[3] From here follows the doctrine of cosmic creation[4] and in particular the emergence of man,[5] with his twin faculties of consciousness and free action,[6] and his social environment.[7]

DOCUMENTARY NOTES

I

We have noted that the conception of Christianity as educative formation made its appearance early. Though 'instruction' had been a common Jewish description for Torah and faith, the Christian use of the word was influenced by the Greek conviction that intellectual culture (paideia) is the supreme human activity. This brought into the faith a gnostic emphasis. True religion means true knowledge, and the Church is called a school.

Preoccupation with true knowledge pervades Christian theology. In a Greek milieu we expect this intellectual emphasis. Salvation is commonly referred to in terms of knowledge (gnosis). In this connection the influence of

Plato is abundantly clear. True knowledge is our end, and it becomes possible only when we get away from the temporal world. Contemplation is prior to action. The true is the good. The ultimately true is God. This intellectualism called for emphasis on logical procedure and 'demonstration'.

Since the Tutor (*paidagogos*) himself has placed us in his Church and set us down before himself, who is the educative and all-knowing Logos, it is only right now at the end of our work to send up to the Lord in due gratitude a fee of praise adequate for such urbane education.

CLEMENT of Alexandria, *The Tutor* 3, 12 (PG 8. 681)

I would make bold to say that it will not just be through a wish for salvation that the true Gnostic will choose *gnosis* and follow it as a means to divine science. For the action of knowing through prolonged discipline becomes perpetual knowledge, and perpetual knowledge becomes by an indissoluble mingling the very essence of the knower and remains a living substance. So if one were to propose to the Gnostic the question as to which he would choose, knowledge of God or eternal salvation, supposing these two to be separate though of course they are absolutely identical, without a moment's delay he would choose knowledge of God, judging as desirable in itself the property of ascending beyond faith through love into knowledge.

CLEMENT of Alexandria, *Miscellanies* 4. 22 (PG 8. 1345)

Gnosis, however, is not limited to rationalist truth. It is essentially revelation, a type of knowledge directly experienced, though approached by symbol and ritual, as in mystery initiation. To this all rational knowledge is only subsidiary. An awareness of these two modes of knowledge is frequent in Christian writers, particularly the mystical ones.

Let us not think that the appearances of the scriptural symbols have been devised as ends in themselves. They have been set up like a screen in front of a knowledge that is ineffable and invisible to the many, thus keeping all-holy things out of reach of the profane. These are disclosed only to geniune lovers of holiness who can lay aside all puerile fantasy before the sacred symbols and who have the requisite simplicity of mind and theoretic faculty to approach that simple and supernal truth residing in the symbols, a truth which surpasses nature. One must remember that there is a double heritage handed down by theologians, on the one hand the ineffable and mystical, on the other the explicit and manifest. The one is of symbols and mysteries, the other of scientific philosophy and demonstration; and both are linked together, the explicit with the mystical. The one uses persuasion and enforces by proof the truth of its statements, the other is a ritual action grounding its truth in God through initiations which admit of no technique.

DIONYSIUS the Pseudo-Areopagite, *Letter* 9 (*PG* 3. 1105)

But human truth had to be recognized as valid once the Aristotelian and Stoic notion of nature *was taken as a norm. This when pursued involved an appreciative attitude to the culture* (paideia) *which the pagans prized as the supreme value.*

Human nature from the beginning has been able, by the conjunction of human reason and divine salvation, to gain knowledge of truth and of the worship due to the one Prince of all things. But malign influence has slipped in and diverted to the making of idols this supreme dignity of man. Since this irregular custom has become ingrained over a long period it presents error to the many as natural and true. The task of the humanist, therefore, and more still of the theologian, is to instruct these people in what they ought to know but have overlooked. Nature alone was sufficient to show them, from the things that cooperate under the arch of heaven, the order of the Demiurge. But a forgetfulness, tolerated by the patience of God, conquered the human mind, playing the villain and transferring on to mere men the name that befits only the true God. Through a few the many have reaped a harvest of evil, blinded by mob custom to the knowledge needed for things firm and immutable. The few who first set up mysteries and liturgies to honour outstanding men engendered in their followers forgetfulness of the viewpoint that is in fact catholic to all men. I myself, though, as I have hinted, my thoughts are those of a theologian, shall speak with the voice of a humanist, setting out to all possessed of intelligence the rule which they should have derived already from the fact of their dependence on the government of the cosmos: that they should hold immutable the cult of God who discerns all things. I do not intend to express this in ornamental speech but shall employ exclusively as argument the study (*historia*) of ancient Greek poetry, written down in books that are the possession of all men without distinction. It was out of these poets that the law of worshipping idols was imposed on the people. A re-reading will serve to convince them of their lack of understanding.

Unknown author (Pseudo-Justin), *On the Monarchy of God* (PG 6. 312)

I imagine it is a point on which all reasonable men would agree that for us culture is the best of all good things. This applies not only to that noble type of education belonging to us Christians which despises all ornament and mere show of words and takes hold only of salvation and the beauty of intellect. It means also the culture of the pagans which the mass of Christians despise as hostile and erroneous and liable to remove people from God. Theirs is an ignorant view. For sky and earth and air and all that is in them are not to be despised just because some people have made a wrong use of them and worshipped these things of God instead of God. Rather, we harvest what is good in these things for life and enjoyment, and what is dangerous we avoid. We do not raise up the creature against the Creator as the foolish do, but from the handicraft we discern the Craftsman, and, as the holy Apostle says, we take prisoner every thought for Christ. . . . So from pagan culture we have accepted whatever promotes enquiry and intellectual contemplation, but whatever leads towards evil spirits and error and the depths of destruction we reject, though it is true that even from the latter we are helped towards the service of God, discerning superior by inferior, and turning the weakness of these pagan things into the strength of our own doctrine. We must not therefore dishonour learning just because some people do. These persons we must regard as perverse and boorish, wanting everyone to be like themselves so as to conceal their own defects in the common reservoir of shortcomings and elude accusations of ignorance. Having agreed on that much for a start let us now go on to look at the life of Basil.

GREGORY of Nazianzus, *In Praise of Saint Basil* (PG 36. 508)

2

Plato's notion of Form as 'that which really is,' and its near relative, Aristotle's notion of Essence or Substance (ousia), were to solve many Christian problems. The latter was particularly helpful in the Trinitarian debates of the fourth century and became of capital importance to the medieval thinkers both Greek and Latin. Likewise the Platonic emphasis on proportion provided the doctrine of analogy, whereby derivatives are referred to a prime unity. Unity dominates the Platonic view of the real.

An Accident is that which cannot exist in itself; it has its existence in another. God, then, is a Substance (*ousia*), and so are his creatures. But God's substance is 'super-substantial' (*hyperousios*).

JOHN DAMASCENE, *Dialectic* (PG 94. 537b)

The fourth sort of likeness is that of species (*eidos*). This likeness is found between image and exemplar, for instance between the picture of an animal and the animal itself. It is in this way that we are said to be like to God. But if we look deeper we shall find that there is a great difference. The picture and the animal participate in their exemplar only by name and shape. But man shares actual reality with God, shares, I mean, in his goodness and wisdom and even in his power. Yet man is not fully like to God. For God is these things by nature and we have them only conditionally (*kata thesin*), and each of us in a different way. Which means that there is immense difference in any comparison with God and even in comparison with one another. The likeness is according to proportion (*analogia*), resembling that of things derived from a single one and compared with it.

JOHN DAMASCENE, *Dialectic* (PG 94. 600a)

The statement 'substance (*ousia*) is a self-existent thing', puzzles the ablest of the philosophers. How can that be self-existent which takes its existence not from itself but from what composes it? They define as self-existent what has its subsistence (*hypostasis*) from itself and does not depend on any superior cause. . . . They divide substance into first and second, and first substance into matter and species; but this does not seem to make the word 'self-existent' any more applicable. For species depend on genera . . . and genera, at least if we follow Plato, depend on Ideas. As for first substance, the individual, comprising matter and species, how can it be self-existent? For, what has matter is nourished by matter; and a thing which modifies species, by happening to be in perpetual flux, will always need a cause to compose it and supply what it loses.

MICHAEL PSELLOS *Scripta Minora*, ed. E. Kurtz and F. Drexl, vol. I, Munich, 1936, p. 451

3

The great campaign in both Judaic and Christian thinking was the defence of monotheism. The Jews had the idea of a transcendent God who could not be discovered by philosophy, for philosophy gleans its harvest from created nature. Here indeed are the two poles of our problem: the one God revealed from beyond nature and the cosmic order philosophically discovered within it. When the Jews were in exile they encountered the Persian doctrine of twin cosmic powers, good and evil. Thereafter the notion of Satan looms large in their tradition. They also came upon the Persian view of intermediary spirits, bad and good. Once angels and mediators appeared on the scene every effort was needed to preserve the worship of the one good God.

The essential separation of Christianity from Judaism occurred on this question of mediation. Christianity postulated the mediator Christ where the Jews had urged direct spontaneous turning to JHWH, the imageless and hidden God. Christians nevertheless wanted also to be monotheistic and here their problem was even greater than the Jewish. For they had somehow to maintain along with monotheism a doctrine of three divine persons, and of the divinity of Jesus, as well as concepts borrowed from Hellenistic Judaism such as logos, angels, wisdom. Here philosophy was summoned as ally. Only dialectic could clear up the intricacies, by distinctions and definitions such as nature and person, hypostatic union, act and potency. The Neoplatonic concept of 'the One' proved invaluable in the effort to build up trinitarian monotheism, and to show the union of Jesus with the Trinity.

Again Celsus goes on: 'If you were to tell Christians that Jesus is not the Son of God, but that God is the universal Father and that he alone is deserving of worship, they still would not agree to omit Jesus from their worship, for he is the leader of their sedition. When they call him Son of God it is not out of any great reverence for God, but because they want to exalt Jesus.'

ORIGEN, *Against Celsus* 8. 14 (PG 11. 1535)

We find a knowledge of the Trinity even among the philosophers of Greece. For they say that their three hypostases exist at once together, with no intermediary between them, and as Mind is related to the First, so, they say, is the third, Soul, related to Mind. And they admit the comparisons of Begotten and Begetter: this we can see from the statement of Plotinus: 'Everything desires its begetter and loves it, especially when begotten and begetter are the same.' (Plotinus, *Enneads* 5. 1. 6, misquoted)

CYRIL of Alexandria, *Against Julian* 8 (PG 76. 920)

Peter and Paul and Barnabas are, with reference to the notion of man, one 'man', and in this sense, as regards being man, they cannot be several. We say they are several only by derivative usage and not by primary usage, and derivative usage can never be preferred, by any man of discernment, to primary. Therefore we must not say about the three persons of the divine essence that they are three gods with reference to the notion of God. For God is one and the same through identity of essence, which, as we have said, is what the word 'God' means.

GREGORY of Nyssa, *On Common Notions* (PG 45. 180)

To this Porphyry bears witness though he raised his voice to attack Christ. The testimonies of our enemies in our favour are strong ones and admit of no refutation. This Porphyry in the second book of his *Various Questions* writes the following words: 'It is not, then, repugnant that a substance may be adopted to complete another substance and to be a part of that substance while yet retaining its own nature after completing the other substance, becoming one with another and yet preserving its own unity. And what is more, without being itself converted it can by its presence convert the things in which it inheres, into its own act.' Porphyry writes this about the union of the soul with the body. Now if this is true of the soul, because of its incorporeality, it is much more true of the divine Word, which is more purely and truly incorporeal. This closes the lips of those who try to attack the union of God with man.

NEMESIUS, *On the Nature of Man* 3 (PG 40. 601)

God is ever in act; just as burning is proper to fire and cooling to snow, so act is to God. All the more so since God is the principle of activity in all other things.

PHILO, *Allegorical Interpretation of the Laws* 1. 3

All the philosophers agree, even without their intending it, when they investigate the first principles of the universe, that God is one. We Christians also affirm that the unified order of the cosmos comes from one God. Why then are they allowed to say and write what they please about the divine, whereas there is a law forbidding us to do so, even though we can advance cogent proofs and reasons for our conviction about the unity of God?

ATHENAGORAS, *Mission on behalf of the Christians*, 7 (PG 6. 904)

4

Granted the idea of one God there was still left for the Christian, as for the Neoplatonist, the task of explaining the phenomenal creation, the world of diversity and change and imperfection. Here Plato's Timaeus, *with its keynote of divine generosity, is very much referred to in Christian tradition, and the doctrine of Ideas, though at times criticized, is influential. The Platonic doctrine of creative emanation involves a notion of 'fall'. If it is adopted it implies that creation is a necessary and eternal activity of God, whereas Christians preferred to link creation, and Fall, with a free act of will.*

The philosophers, plagiarizing Moses, held that the world was created. So Plato clearly asks: 'Is it true that the world had no beginning of its existence, or did it derive its existence from some beginning? Being visible, it is tangible, and being tangible it has a body.' And when he says that 'it is difficult to find the maker and father of the universe' he implies not only that the universe was generated but that it was generated as a son. The term 'father' is used because the world derives its being from him alone and is made out of nothing. The Stoics too hold that the world was created.

CLEMENT of Alexandria, *Miscellanies* 5. 14 (PG 8. 136)

Since the world shows such variety and holds such a great diversity of rational beings what other cause can we assign for its existence except diverse grades and differences in the lapse of those beings which emanate from the original unity?

ORIGEN, *On First Principles* 2. 1. 1. (PG 11. 182)

The universe which consists of heaven and earth is also called *cosmos* (order, ornament), as Paul says: 'The form of this *kosmos* passes away' (1 *Cor.* 7. 31). But Our Lord and Saviour refers to another world, one which is difficult to describe and picture for it is beyond this visible world. His words 'I am not of this world' imply that he was of some other world. As we have said, it is difficult to describe that other world; if we attempted it we should run the risk of giving some people the notion that we accept the existence of those imaginary forms which the Greeks call 'ideas'. It is not in keeping with our doctrine to talk about an incorporeal world that exists only in the mind or in the flimsy realm of pure thought. I do not see how we could say that our Saviour came from such an ideal world or that the saints will go to it.

But there is no doubt that the Saviour refers to something more glorious and splendid than the present world: he invites and urges all his believers to direct their minds towards it. But it is uncertain whether the world he directs us towards is far apart and separate from this world in space and quality and splendour. I prefer to think that it is superior to this world in quality and splendour but is nevertheless situated within the confines of the present universe. But this question is beyond the mind and thought of men.

ORIGEN, *On First Principles* 2. 3. 6 (*PG* 11. 195)

A certain heretic, Hermogenes, thinking he was putting forward a very new idea, said that God made all things out of a sort of matter which was as eternal and ungenerated as himself. His reason was that God could not make generated things out of the non-existent, and that as God is eternally ruler and creator matter is eternally his servant and eternally generated; but not all of it . . . for he took some of it and tamed it and the rest he allowed to stay in wild disorder. That which he tamed Hermogenes holds to be the cosmos, and the untamed is just unordered matter. . . . Hermogenes, it seems, was not aware that all this is found in the Socratic myth which Plato works out so much more fully than he does.

HIPPOLYTUS, *Philosophic Refutation of All Heresies* 8. 17, ed. Wendland, Leipzig, 1916, p. 236

5

The inner essence of life resists philosophic explanation. Life, being a process of pure succession, cannot be genuinely analysed as if it had juxtaposed parts. A pure continuity is negated by any division. Psychic states are not quantitative. Life is associated with being and unity, but its other association, with

*time and diversity, made it a perpetual puzzle for the Greek philosophers.
The word 'soul' is among the most frequent in their literature.*

*They constantly describe it in terms of the alien criteria of spatial content
or separation. The soul is in the body. This notion, found in the primitive
cults and poetry, is retained by the philosophers. The soul is something 'from
without' which can exist independently. The consequent doctrine of immortality was one of the most important legacies of Greek thought to Christian.
The Jewish legacy had been rather that of the resurrection of the body. The
separation and salvation of soul from body was very feasible given the Platonist conception of the body as tomb (sōma sēma), and it was tempting to
follow Plato into theories of pre-existence and transmigration. With Aristotle's hylomorphic notion of soul, as the* form *of the body, the separation
was harder to argue, without invoking the scholastic and rather un-Aristotelian*
forma separabilis, *which restores Form to its Platonic aloofness.*

*It was difficult to explain transition from the divine stability to the temporal
mobility of life. Yet life could not be totally denied to the divine perfection.
The Platonists came to speak of the ideas of the Mind-World (kosmos
noētos) as being 'awake and alive'. Idea is in a sense a thinking as well as a
thought. Aristotle's Thought of Thought, like Plato's Form of the Good,
is remote from human life, though Aristotle's notion of active intellect (nous
poietikos) in man is an attempt at vital connection between divine and human.
The latter notion was of great use to Christians in their doctrine of divine
illumination: active intellect means a sharing in the divine, whereby man is
made in the image of God. Soul is a part of the harmonious cosmos.*

*Soul then is a unitive form. Its freedom of will is essentially an urge to
unity, conquering the complexity of movement and plurality. The essential
self, where the whole personality is a simple state, is not determined, physically
or psychologically. This gives an existential unity of action, a creative urge
of simple direction, like a single wave pushing past many obstacles. The
philosopher's search is for the pure self, the deeper self, the free self, the monad
self. In typical Greek fashion the Christian thinkers tied the notion of free will
to that of intellect: where there is the power to distinguish and deliberate there
is the consequent power to choose.*

Contemporary with the divine thought we were made God's children,
set in the best and most stable situation by his orderly rule, which, for
the sake of man, first of all acts on the universe and the heaven and the
solar orbit and the circles of the stars, and then attends to man himself,
expending on him the greatest care. Considering man the most important work, the divine rule has guided his soul with prudence and wisdom

and tempered his body with beauty and harmony, and has breathed into the actions of humanity their regulative and ordering element.

CLEMENT of Alexandria, *The Tutor* 1. 2 (PG 8. 256)

Iamblichus . . . says that each type of living creature has its own proper type of soul. That is why he wrote a book to prove that there can be no transmigration of soul from man to brute nor from brute to man, but only from beast to beast and from human to human. For this reason Iamblichus more than any other writer seems to me to have arrived at Plato's real opinion and also at the truth of the matter.

NEMESIUS, *On the Nature of Man* 2. 18 (PG 40. 584)

Animate things are moved from within themselves, for an image springs up in them which incites to effort. In certain animals the images which arise and stimulate effort are of such a nature that they motivate in an orderly manner; in the spider, for instance, there arises the image of weaving, and the effort to weave follows, imaginative nature inciting the insect to work in orderly fashion. Over and above this imaginative nature an insect is not considered to have any other faculty. In the bee there is simply the imaginative instinct which makes it collect honey.

The rational animal, however, has a power other than its imaginative nature; it has reason, which is able to evaluate the images which arise, disapproving of some and accepting others, so that the animal may be guided according to these images. Therefore, since the nature of reason allows the contemplation of good and evil, by following this nature we can, after seeing good and evil objects, select the one and avoid the other. So we merit praise when we practise the good and blame when we do the reverse. . . . To be affected by some external cause which arouses this image or that is admittedly not one of those things over which we have control. But to determine that we shall employ the affection this way or that is the prerogative of reason alone within us, which according to the alternative impressions, directs us to what is good and fitting or turns us aside to what is the opposite. If anyone holds that it is impossible for us to resist the external stimulus, let him attend to his own feeling and movements and see whether there is not in his controlling principle of reason, an approval and assent and inclination directing him through specious reasonings to a certain action. . . . To say that our actions are determined by external objects and to detach all blame from ourselves by declaring that we are like

83

pieces of wood or stone dragged about by external influences, is not in conformity with reason and is the statement of a man whose only wish is to destroy the whole idea of free will. . . . The onus is on ourselves to lead a good life. It is not the task of God who asks it of us, nor is it something imposed on us by external agents. Neither is it, as some think, the operation of fate. It is our own task.

ORIGEN, *On First Principles* 3. 1. 2–6 (*PG* 11. 249)

If man can initiate none of his own actions human deliberation is pointless. What use is deliberating if a man is not master of any of his deeds? Yet it would be absurd to think that such a fair and worthy human accomplishment as deliberation is useless. Now all deliberation is with a view to doing something: action is its purpose. Another argument is this: when we possess certain powers of action we must also have control of the actions that deploy these powers. And as we possess the powers needed for certain virtues, the virtues themselves must also be within our power. . . . If repetition of action forms habit and is due to our own initiative then the habit itself is within our power. And if habits are within our power then the actions that come from them are also in our power. . . . It is up to us to become good men or bad, just as we choose.

NEMESIUS of Emesa, *On the Nature of Man* 39 (*PG* 40. 764)

6

Mimesis *gives the key to norms of action. Man, like the rest of the moving universe in the* Timaeus, *has to imitate, as well as he may, the divine stability. From study of mathematics, and especially astronomy, man can grasp the idea of cosmic harmony and law. This cosmic law becomes the 'natural law' of the Stoics, and right action means living ever in agreement with it. In Hellenistic Judaism and then in Christianity the revealed law of God is equated with this philosophic natural law. Thus 'nature' (physis) remains in Christian teaching as ethical norm. An action is wrong if it is 'unnatural'. Here, as in so much other Christian thought, is the Platonic postulate that a ready-made rule is objectively given to our mind before action begins. The teleological ethic of Aristotle, so much adopted by Christianity, is but a version of Platonic mimesis.*

Mimesis *is also the rule of art. Nature herself is an artist that copies God 'as far as possible' and man in his turn may copy nature's art. A work of art is an outer image of the divine and an outer gate of access to the divine. The Christian veneration of images relied on this conception, borrowed from Plato's 'Form of the Good'. Icon connects the soul with Archetype.*

Plato had of course depreciated art as being too far removed from Reality, 'a copy of a copy'. Something of this affected Christian writing. Drama and poetry, and belles-lettres generally, were rather discouraged in the Christian centuries.

Plato's notion of the Good, or Aristotle's of 'happiness' (eudaimonia) through contemplation (theoria), as the final purpose of all action and making, became for Christian thought the 'beatific vision' of Paradise, Dante's 'good of the intellect'.

No one whether he is Jew or Gentile lacks the law which is in men by nature. . . . God implanted in man the faculty of reason which tells him what he must do and what he must avoid, and this faculty is conferred on all men alike. . . . This natural law speaks to all who are subject to it; only infants, it seems, who have not yet the power of distinguishing right from wrong, are exempt from the enactments of natural law.

ORIGEN, *Commentary on 'Romans'* 3. 6 (PG 14. 938)

The action of the Word does not produce poets. It does not train philosophers or orators. But its educative power is of such a nature as to make mortals become immortal and humans to become divine; and dwellers on earth it transforms into dwellers above Olympus.

Unknown author (Pseudo-Justin), *Discourse* 5 (PG 6. 237)

The beauty of the vision of God is so great and so desirable that Plotinus unhesitatingly says (*Enneads* 1. 6. 7) that the man who enjoys all other goods in abundance, and has not this, is supremely miserable.

AUGUSTINE, *City of God* 10. 16: Migne, *Patrologia Latina*, vol. 41, col. 293

7

Ancient thinkers could envisage man only in relation to his society. The supremacy of the individual does not flower until the Renaissance. Plato cannot enquire into human goodness or justice without looking at the social model where he may find these values 'writ large'. His emphasis on pure intellect makes him imagine a thought-society 'laid up in heaven' as model for the soul's justice. So Christians came to see the heavenly Jerusalem, the civitas dei, *in Platonic terms. The Neoplatonists could picture their divine Nous, the hypostatic harmony of all ideas, as a well-ordered city and fatherland. 'This heaven has no other where than the Divine Mind' (Dante, Par 27. 110). Hellenistic Jews saw the Platonic Ideas as Angel citizens, so Christians interpreted redemption to mean that men could be co-opted to fill the places of the Angels who had 'fallen' from the fatherland of Idea.*

The besetting social problem of Christendom was the ever growing division between sacred and secular. In ancient Israel Church and State were one; Jahweh ruled, in concrete reality, 'a people and a land'. But in Christian Europe the city 'laid up in heaven' has been beleaguered from the 'city of the world'. Perhaps this was inevitable when the destruction of Jerusalem forced Jews as well as Christians to live in lands that did not belong to them, amid alien society. Yet a prime religious yearning of man has always been for an integral community where the Church is the State and the State is the people. This was achieved in Christianity only in the monastic orders, not in the greater society. Outside the cloister the schism remained. The separation of Church and State was embodied in the law codes of the Christian Empire and became a commonplace of medieval thought. At the end of the medieval Greek tradition it affects Gemistos Plethon into reviving again a Platonic scheme of the state with ancient religion (Hellenismos) built into it as in the Neoplatonic experiment of Julian. He criticizes Christian monks for their neglect of political duty: they are 'sophists', false philosophers, unlike those of Plato. Plethon is a product of the growing rift between sacred and secular and in a way is a Greek parallel to Machiavelli.

The influence of Plato is felt all through Christian social and political thought, whether men considered the eternity of the heavenly city or the genesis of the earthly.

Because we need the arts and sciences and the useful things they produce we need one another. And because we need one another we form one large assembly together and there in the business of living we share out the things necessary to life. To this assembling and living together we have given the name of city. In it we benefit one another by staying close together without any need to travel. Man is by nature a gregarious being made for society, made for citizenship. No individual is completely self-sufficient. Clearly then cities exist for the sake of human intercourse and learning.

NEMESIUS, *On the Nature of Man* I. 6 (*PG* 40. 520)

The Platonic political model was the Mind–Cosmos of Forms, a diversity brought by harmony into unity, the things of earth re-ordered to match the order of the stars. The Platonists loved to repeat a political maxim from Homer: 'The rule of many is not good: one ruler let there be.' The philosopher-king is trained to penetrate into that divine unity, and then his citizens can share, by imitation (mimesis), *his union with the divine.*

The greatest blessings of mankind are the divine gifts which have been granted to us by the sublime mercy of God – the priesthood and the imperial authority. The priesthood ministers to things divine, the imperial authority is set over and shows diligence in things human. Both proceed from one and the same source, and both adorn the life of man.... If the priesthood be entirely without blame, and full of faith before God, and if the imperial authority rightly and duly adorns the commonwealth in its charge, there will follow a happy concord to benefit mankind.

JUSTINIAN, *Novellae vi*, Preface, ed. R. Schoell and G. Kroll, Berlin, 1895

When a prince rules himself, then you may be sure that he really rules his subjects; for when they see that the ruler set over them is master of his passions and pleasures they will be moved by their own desire and free will to submit themselves. But if they see him a slave to pleasure and passions they will think it intolerable to be the slaves of a slave.

PHOTIUS, *Letter to Prince Michael* 57 (*PG* 102. 627 ff.)

Cycles of time produce, and will always produce, similar ways of life and similar activities from age to age. Nothing new has ever yet come into existence: nothing comes into existence which has not existed as the same in idea at some time in the past, and which will not also exist again at some time in the future. No nation is a disbeliever in the existence of God; but different men have different and discrepant opinions of the nature of deity.... I follow the opinion of the school of Zoroaster, as being the best; it agrees with that of Pythagoras and Plato; it is more genuine than all others and it is the traditional religion of us Greeks.

GEMISTOS PLETHON, *On Laws* 3. 43, ed. C. Alexandre, Paris, 1858, p. 256

You, gods, have granted that by goodness to our kinsfolk and to all mankind we may imitate you who are always the source of good things and never of evil. You have also granted that by civil association with one another we can share the blessing of resembling you, as far as we may. You are all born of the same father, Zeus our King, all begotten of him alone, and you yourselves have unity and community with one another in the highest.

GEMISTOS PLETHON, *On Laws* 3. 34, ed. C. Alexandre, Paris, 1858, p. 186

Remember that being a king is like steering a ship. On a ship if a sailor makes a mistake he does not inflict great damage on the crew. But if the captain makes a mistake he causes the loss of the whole vessel. Similarly if a citizen goes astray he does not harm the state so much as himself. But if the king errs he causes injury to the whole kingdom. . . . Pay attention, then, to how the wheel of human affairs keeps turning, ever changing things round. Despite its rapid change keep your own pious contemplation immovable. To change along with the changes of these things is sign of an unsure mind. Stand firm, wholly based on the Good.

Romance of Barlaam and Joasaph, ed. Boissonade, Paris, 1832, p. 332

So the main topics of pagan thought were found to be fertile ground for Christian thinking. Truth and faith, knowledge and being, God and creation, world and matter, mind and will, good and evil, person and city – on all these matters pagan philosophy was able to contribute. And the whole historical process we have been contemplating, the symbiosis of philosophy and faith, was found itself to have theological significance. Through it the original Jewish preaching of Jesus was made beneficiary of the total Greek intellectual achievement, and Christians gratefully saw this legacy as the loving work of Providence 'preparing for the Gospel'.

Thus arose Christian thought, the existence of which faces the historian as a European fact. But the historian is not content to state the fact; he wants to penetrate to explanation. *If he starts from the Greeks he cannot resist the impression that the philosophy in Christianity is the philosophy of the Greeks and that Christianity did not really construct a philosophy of its own. Indeed the Greek philosophy which it borrowed during the patristic and medieval centuries eventually provided material to men like Galileo and Descartes for a new secular conception of the universe and of man. It is arguable that Greek philosophy had always been rather a foreign body within the Christian religion. The logos which the young Augustine thought he found in the Gospel was really the cosmic reason of the Stoics, and later he himself felt bound to reject two of its corollaries, the eternity of the world and the eternal pre-existence of the soul. Again in the thirteenth century Aquinas attempted a new synthesis wherein philosophy could be the handmaid of faith and yet be declared autonomous. Aquinas had at this stage before him the translated works of Aristotle, an admirable product of the Hellenic talent of conceptual precision. But it was difficult to apply to these works his basic principle that truth does not contradict truth, that reason does not really oppose faith. There were Aristotelian ideas such as the limited nature of the cosmos, the eternity of the world, the identity of human intellects, where it was troublesome to apply the magisterial criterion of faith clearly and easily; and anyway to do so was rather to cancel the autonomy of reason. The guidance of philosophy by faith was therefore precarious.*

At the Renaissance the medieval synthesis between Judaeo-Christian belief and Hellenic rationalism was more and more Socratically examined. The synthesis tended to fall apart. The Reformers tended to go back to the primitive biblical faith, and the rationalist philosophers went their own way. Then, after the Renaissance some of the basic contradictions between Aristotelianism and Christian belief were triumphantly disclosed by an advancing rationalism. The element of belief was rubbed away. Pascal rightly observed how God meant only a chiquenaude *for Descartes, whose rationalism was self-reliant and no longer needed the tutelage of faith.*

The historian's inner view of the synthesis might thus be that the combination was artificial and unstable. But the fact under review is a complex one and it now seems wise to try and exemplify what a rich variety of historical opinion it can stimulate.

Part Two
Historical Approaches to the Synthesis

In the ages of faith the chronicler accepted that the origin of Christian faith was a divine phenomenon. But the modern historian, shy of appearing theological, asserts that he has no method of assessing divine phenomena. It takes him all his time to explain human phenomena by human factors. And he sees that Christian origins do present him with human manifestations such as this assimilation of pagan philosophy. His approach to evidence will inevitably depend very much on where his own sympathy lies. He may of course find it possible to view the issue with a certain neutrality.

1 E. R. DODDS

The historian's interpretation of this period is inevitably coloured in some degree by his own religious beliefs. It is therefore right that I should declare my interest, so that readers may make the appropriate allowances. It is in fact a kind of disinterest. As an agnostic I cannot share the standpoint of those who see the triumph of Christianity as the divine event to which the whole creation moved. But equally I cannot see it as the blotting out of the sunshine of Hellenism by what Proclus called 'the barbarian theosophy'. If there is more about pagans in these lectures than about Christians, it is not because I like them better; it is merely because I know them better. I stand outside this particular battle, though not above it: I am interested less in the issues which separated the combatants than in the attitudes and experiences which bound them together.

Pagan and Christian in an Age of Anxiety, Cambridge, 1965, p. 5

But some historians refuse to be neutral. They argue that historical explanation lies below the surface of cultural expression, whether religious or philosophic, that it lies in commerce and society. Ideology yields to economics. There were on the ancient scene the educated rich of the commercial cities, and there were the proletarian poor. *The urban rich cultivated philosophy, seeking its advice on the proper use of wealth or the staying power to maintain it through position and class. But as their political power declined they turned more and more to philosophies of after-life or moral theories, which deteriorated into mere beliefs about supermen or even into sorcery and magic. Here they were easily fitted into Christianity, which had started as a communist move-ment among dispossessed proletarians but now shifted its emphasis to accommo-date the rich. The imperial sceptre was passing from educated to uneducated, from upper classes to proletariat. Thus change of cultural idiom is seen as accessory to social and economic movement.*

Historians with this approach are unaffected by the problem of origins. If they find that neither the pagan nor the Christian evidence throws much light on the historical person of Jesus, they are not upset; for them the social environment is more important than the person. For they postulate that it is society which produces both personality and documents, and since each succes-sive generation and sect of Christianity has managed to create a Founder in its own image and likeness, we are to assume that the first generation did no better.

About the pagan society our socialist historian takes particular note of the landholders with their slave ownership and economic reliance on slave produc-tivity. Slave productivity tended to be technically inferior, and this was the cause of political and economic decline. Alongside this there was the troubled class division of patricians and plebeians, with the former controlling trade and political procedure. All this contributed to the emergence of imperial absolutism. There was a weakening too of social ties, though with this came a more general humanitarian idealism. Commercial travel produced an international mentality: men were easily detached from local allegiances and cults and were ready to embrace novelties. Under the Empire increased credulity characterized the proletarian mind. There was a growing religiosity, tending towards monotheism. Everything, then, indicated a society ready to submit to a new universalist religion. Over against this state of affairs in the Empire the historian notes the development in Judaism from local state to universal diaspora. The Jewish condition of international exile became irreversible when a final resurgence of nationalist hope was quashed by the Roman destruction of Jerusalem in A.D. 70. It is no accident that the rise of Christianity as a universal creed is centred round this latter event.

Christianity, then, appears to such historians as a proletarian movement prompted by economic and social distress, buoyed up religiously by the dynamic social gospel of Jesus which condemned the 'rulers of the people' and found expression in the communism of the first Christian group in Jerusalem. The *communism was to fail later when the movement gained size and fell under the control of a bureaucracy drawn from the administrative class of the Empire.*

The proletarian Christian group had been strictly organized with religious discipline from the very beginning, but its organization was to develop in a new way through the influence of the ruling classes. The key to the development is the office of bishop. At first the bishop had the merely ad hoc *function of 'supervising' the deacons who administered material relief among the community. But economic function is the one which always naturally comes to dominate. Bishops soon relegated to subordination and unimportance the inspired prophetic teachers who had at first held the place of honour in the meetings. A bishop's primary skill was economic, not prophetic. So bishops eventually became men of extensive property and social importance, and their office attracted able candidates from the imperial civil service.*

The original Christian organization had been proletarian in origin and hated the rich. It was not communist in the modern sense, for its communism was not based upon community of production but upon community of consumption. Indeed it despised labour, the basis of productivity, and expected a Kingdom of God on this earth in which the wealth of the rich, however dubiously produced, would anyhow be shared out evenly. The community at first allied itself with the rebel instinct of Judaism, but the execution of the founder made it necessary to exploit the Jewish belief in resurrection. As the movement became international this tendency appealed also to the pagan proletariat. Its primitive communism was, alas, doomed to decline; prophets, teachers and congregation submitted to the bureaucracy of bishops. Monasticism and local heresies fought hard to revive the original communism, but, as Church and State coalesced into a new dyarchy, the effort failed. The clergy became 'a congregational bureaucracy headed by the bishop', and the bishops tended to be chosen from among the administrative educated class, 'sober, business-like, practical men'.

A typical exponent of this sort of history is Kautsky (1854–1938), the influential Marxist historian of socialism.

2 KARL JOHANN KAUTSKY

Philosophy developed only in the great commercial centres, but only in those where there were elements outside of commerce who were assured of leisure and freedom by their property or their social position. In many Greek trading cities such elements were the great landowners, who were relieved of work by their slaves and did not live in the country, but in the city, so that they avoided falling into the boorishness of the country squire but felt all the influences of the city and its great commerce.

It would seem however that such a class of landholders, living in the city and philosophizing, appeared only in maritime cities whose land area was large enough to produce such a landed aristocracy, but not large enough to keep them from the city and tie their interests down to extending their land holdings. These conditions are to be seen above all in the Greek maritime cities. The lands of the Phoenician cities by the sea were too small to produce such landed property; everybody lived by trade.

In cities surrounded by extensive territories, the landholders seem to have remained more under the influence of country life, to have developed further towards the mentality of the country squire. In the great inland trading centres of Asia, the group who were most free from working for a living and least engaged in practical activities were the priests of certain shrines. Quite a few of these shrines won importance and wealth enough to maintain permanent priests, whose duties were light enough. The same social task that fell to the share of the aristocracy in the Greek seaside towns was incumbent on the priests of the temples in the great trade centres of the Oriental mainland, in particular Egypt and Babylon: that is, the development of scientific thought, of philosophy. This however set a limit to Oriental thinking from which Greek thought was free: constant connection with and regard for a religious cult. The cult gained what philosophy lost, and the priests gained too. In Greece the priests remained simple officials of the rites, guardians of the shrines and performers of the religious acts there; in the great commercial centres of the Orient they became preservers and administrators of all of knowledge, scientific as well as social, mathematics, astronomy and medicine as well as history and law. Their influence in the state and society was enormously increased by this. Religion itself however was able to attain a spiritual depth of which the Greek mythology was not capable, since Hellenic philosophy soon put this to one side, without trying to fill out its naïve intuitions with deeper knowledge, and to reconcile the two. [pp. 168–9]

Natural philosophy began in the cities, but gradually many of these cities grew so large that their inhabitants began to get out of touch with nature and lose interest in her. More and more the cities took the leading role in the spiritual and economic life of extensive regions; and this development, as we have seen, dissolved all the social support that the individual had previously found in traditional organizations and ways of thought. In addition, it intensified the class contradictions and gave rise to bitterer class conflicts, leading sometimes to the overthrow of all hitherto accepted social relationships. It was now society, rather than nature, that kept bringing new surprises to men in the great cities and setting them new tasks every day, every day raising the question: what is to be done?

It was not the reasons why things happened in nature that were uppermost in men's minds now, but the question of what they ought to do in society: not the knowledge of necessary natural connections, but the apparently free postulation of new social purposes. Ethics replaced natural philosophy, and took the form of the quest for the supreme happiness of the individual. This had already been so in the Hellenic world after the Persian wars. The Roman world, we have seen, was but a plagiarist of the Greeks in art and science; they got their treasures by plunder, not by work, in the intellectual realm as well as the material. The Romans got to know Greek philosophy at a time when the ethical interest outweighed the interest in the knowledge of nature. Accordingly Roman thought too did not concern itself much with natural philosophy and turned its attention immediately to ethics.

In the first centuries of the Empire two tendencies in the wisdom of life dominated philosophical thought: the doctrine of Epicurus and Stoicism.

Epicurus called philosophy an activity that brings about a happy life by means of concepts and proofs. He believed this would be achieved by striving for pleasure, but only for rational lasting enjoyment, not for transitory sensual dissipations, which lead to the loss of health and wealth, and hence to pain.

This was a philosophy very well suited to a class of exploiters that found no other employment for their wealth than to consume it. What they needed was a rational regulation of the life of enjoyment. But this theory gave no consolation to those, and their number kept growing, who had already suffered bodily, spiritual or financial shipwreck; nor to the poor and wretched, nor to the satiated, those who were revolted by pleasures. And not to those who still had an interest in the traditional forms of the community and still followed goals beyond their own personality, those patriots who grieved to see the decline of state and society, without being able to prevent it. For all these groups the pleasures of this world seemed stale and vain. They turned to the Stoic doctrine, which valued not pleasure but virtue as the highest good, as the only blessedness, and held external goods, health, wealth, etc., to be matters just as indifferent as external evils.

This ended by leading many people to turn away from the world altogether, to despise life, even to long for death. Suicide became common in Imperial Rome; it actually became fashionable.

But it was remarkable that, along with the longing for death, a real terror of death grew up in Roman society. . . . There arose a fear of death such as antiquity had never known before. Cowardice took root; death became a bugbear, instead of the brother of sleep that he had been.

More and more men felt the need of a doctrine that would assert the immortality of the individual, not as an unessential shadow but as a blissful being. Soon bliss was no longer sought in earthly pleasure, not even in earthly virtue, but in the attainment of a better world beyond, for which this wretched life is but a preparation. This conception found strong support in Plato's doctrine, and that was the way in which the Stoic school too developed.

Plato had already taught of a life beyond, in which the souls freed from their bodies lived on and received rewards and punishments for their deeds on earth. In the thirteenth chapter of the tenth book of his *Republic* he tells of a Pamphylian who had fallen in war. On the twelfth day after his death, as he was about to be cremated, he suddenly awoke and related how his soul, after leaving his body, had come to a wondrous place where there were fissures, part leading to heaven, part to the inner parts of the earth. There judges sat in judgement on the souls that came, showing the just the way to the right to heaven, where inconceivable beauty holds sway, and pointing out to the unjust the way down on the left into the bowels of the earth, into a subterranean abyss, where they must make good their earthly sins tenfold. The incurably wicked are seized by wild men, fiery to behold, and chained and tortured. For the others, however, in the abyss, and for those in heaven, a new life begins after a thousand years. The Pamphylian, who had seen all this, had been charged to relate it and brought to life again by a miracle.

Who can help thinking here of heaven and hell in the Christian sense, the sheep on the right hand and the goats on the left, the everlasting fire prepared in Hell (*Matthew* 25, verses 33 and 41), and the dead who lived again 'until the thousand years were finished' (*Revelation* 20, verse 5), and so forth? And yet Plato lived in the fourth century B.C.

It sounds equally Christian when we read the following: 'The body is the soul's burden and punishment. It weighs down on the soul and keeps it in bonds.' It was not a Christian who wrote this, however, but the Stoic philosopher Seneca, teacher and minister of Nero, the persecutor of Christians.

Another passage has a similar sound: 'By this carcass the soul is hidden, varnished over, contaminated, separated from what is true and its own, cast into deception; its whole battle is against the burdensome flesh. It strives thither, to the place from which it was sent forth: there eternal rest awaits it; after this massive and confused world it beholds the pure and clear.'

Seneca is not the only philosopher of his time who formulated or used expressions that sound Christian to us.

In the particular, the ideas we are now dealing with, the immortality of the soul and the beyond, had any number of adherents in the era of the origin of Christianity. Thus for example, the Alexandrian Jew Philo, who lived at the beginning of our era, ended his first book on the allegories of the holy laws with the sentence: 'True, Heraclitus has said, "We live their [the gods'] death and die their life"; when we are alive, the soul is dead and buried in the body as in a funeral mound, while the soul lives its own life when we are dead, and is freed from the evil and the corpse of the life tied to the body.'

More and more, preparation for the life to come seemed far more important than the fight for the goods of this world. But how was it to be found? Formerly the citizen had had three clear and reliable guides to action in tradition, the will of the people and the needs of the community. These were gone now. Tradition had become an empty shadow; the people no longer felt it had a common will; the needs of the community had become a matter of indifference. The individual stood helpless, abandoned to himself, in the stream of new ideas and new relations pouring into society, and looked around for a new firm point of support, for teachings and teachers that would teach truth and the right wisdom of life, and show him the right way to the kingdom of God. As always, when a new need arises, there were many men who sought to satisfy it. They began to preach an individual morality, a morality by means of which the individual, without any change in society, would rise out of and above this world and become a worthy citizen of a better one.

What else could rhetorical and philosophical ability resort to? All political activity had come to an end; interest in the study of the causes of things, scientific activity had broken down. What other outlet was left for the energy of orators and philosophers than to try cases for the winning of property or teach the morality of despising property, to become a preacher or a jurist? And in fact both of these fields were well cultivated in the days of the Empire, and the Romans made notable contributions in the form of declamations on the nullity of the goods of this world as well as in paragraphs on the defence of these same goods. It became the fashion to make edifying speeches and make up and compile edifying sayings and anecdotes. At bottom the gospels are nothing more than a reworking of this sort of collections of sayings and anecdotes.

There were now moral preachers for every class, undertaking to raise men to greater moral completeness on the pattern of their own sublime personality. For the proletariat, philosophers of the Cynic school presented themselves, disciples of the notorious Diogenes; these men preached in the streets, lived by begging, and saw happiness in dirt and freedom from needs, which liberated them from any work; work they hated and despised as grievous sin. Christ and his apostles too are presented as begging street preachers. None of the gospels has anything to do with work. For all their contradictions they are in accord on that point.

The nobles however had their own house moralists, belonging to the Stoic school for the most part.

'After the fashion of the powerful since the time of the Scipios, Augustus had his own philosopher around in the person of Areus, a Stoic from Alexandria; to him he intrusted Livia to derive consolation after the death of her son Drusus. Augustus had Areus in his suite when he entered Alexandria after the battle of Actium and told his fellow-citizens, in the speech in which he pardoned the Alexandrians for their support of Marc Antony, that Areus was one of the reasons for his mildness. Spiritual guides of the same sort in other palaces and houses cared for the spiritual needs of the mighty. Formerly teachers of a new theory, they were for the Romans, after the civil wars, practical shepherds of souls, spiritual directors, consolers in misfortune, confessors. They accompanied the victims of the Emperor's arbitrary will to their deaths, and gave them the last cheering words. Canus Julius, who received his death sentence by the Emperor Caligula with thanksgiving and died with calm and composure, was accompanied by 'his philosopher' on his last march. When Thrasea went into the room in which he had his veins opened, he was accompanied by his son-in-law Helvidius and by the Cynic Demetrius, as chaplain, and in the torments of the slow death kept his eyes on Demetrius' (B. Bauer, *Christus und die Cäsaren*, p. 22 f.).

Thus even before the rise of Christianity we see the father confessor appear on the stage and a new historical factor enter into the countries of Europe, theocracy, not because of the teachings of a single man, but in virtue of the new conditions. There had long been priests among the Romans and Greeks, of course, but they had small importance in the state. It was only under the Empire that there arose in the countries of Europe the conditions for a theocracy such as was known in early antiquity in many lands of the Orient. Now there took form in the West as well the preconditions for a spiritual caste, a priestly order as ruler of men, already marked by the presence in so many of its members of the sanctimoniousness and arrogance which are characteristic of the priesthood and which from that day to this have earned it the enmity of any elements of society with strength enough not to need a guardian.

Plato had declared that the state would only be well-ordered when philosophers ruled it and the rest of the citizens had nothing to do with it. Now his dream was realized, in a way which would not have been much to his taste.

But these moral preachers and father confessors were not enough for this unstable generation. The state was in uncontrollable decline. The barbarians were knocking more and more loudly at the doors of the Empire, which was often torn by the bloody rivalries of its generals. And the misery of the masses grew; depopulation increased. Roman society saw its own decline, but it was a generation too corrupt, too sick in body and mind, too cowardly, too much at odds with itself and its surroundings to make an energetic attempt to free itself from its intolerable conditions. It had lost faith in itself, and the only support that kept it from total desperation was hope in help from a higher power, from a saviour.

At first this saviour was seen in the Caesars. At the time of Augustus a prophecy, of the Sibylline books, circulated, which predicted a saviour in the near future. People saw Augustus as a prince of peace who would lead the Empire, torn by the civil wars, into a new epoch of glamour and prosperity, where there would be 'peace on earth to men of good will'.

But the Caesars brought neither lasting peace nor an economic or moral uplift, despite all the confidence men had in their divine powers. And that was not a little.

People regarded them as gods; even before the doctrine of God's becoming man arose, the doctrine of a man's becoming a god was accepted, and yet this second procedure must obviously be much more difficult than the first.

Where all political life has been wiped out, the head of the state rises so high above the populace that he is a sort of superman, compared to them, since he unites in his own person the entire power and might of society and directs it wherever he desires. On the other hand, the deities were regarded as very human in antiquity. Thus the leap from superman to god was not too violent. [pp. 88–97]

Keen observation and inquiry into natural philosophy and into the causes of events was refined, as we have seen, as cities arose. The urban observers were now able to discover impersonal events in nature, so simple and yet so rigorously regular that they could easily be recognized as necessary, beyond the realm of the capriciousness that is bound up with the notion of personal deities. Above all it was the motions of the heavenly bodies that gave rise to the concept of regularity and necessity. Natural science begins with astronomy. Then these concepts are extended to all of nature; men begin to look for necessary, regular connections everywhere. The regularly recurring experience is the basis of this activity.

The picture changes when, for the reasons mentioned, interest in scientific study of nature wanes and is replaced by ethical interest. The human spirit is now no longer concerned with such simple motions as the paths of the stars, which he could take as his starting point; he deals exclusively with himself, with the phenomenon which is most complicated, most variable, most elusive, which most resists scientific study. And then ethics no longer has to do with knowing what is and has been, what is present in experience, and for the most part in regularly repeated experience; instead it deals with desires and duties for the future, which lies before us not yet experienced and hence seemingly in complete freedom. Here wishing and dreaming have full scope, and fantasy runs wild, rising above all the confines of experience and criticism. Lecky is right in saying in his *History of the Rise and Influence of Rationalism in Europe* (New York, 1866, I, 43): 'The philosophy of Plato, by greatly aggrandizing the sphere of the spiritual, did much to foster the belief (in sorcery); and we find that whenever, either before or after the

Christian era, that philosophy has been in the ascendant, it has been accompanied by a tendency to magic.'

At the same time life in the large city robs the inhabitants, who are now the intellectual leaders, of contact with nature, and the need and possibility of observing and understanding nature. The notion of what is natural and what is possible becomes weaker for them; they lose their measuring-rod for the absurdity of the impossible and unnatural or supernatural.

The more helpless the individual feels, the more desperately he gropes for solid support in some personality standing out beyond the ordinary: the more desperate the conditions and the greater the need for miracles, the more he will be inclined to lay miracles to the account of that personality, whom he regards as his rescuer and saviour: in fact he will demand miracles as the touchstone which proves that the saviour is genuine. [pp. 100–1]

It was not from the Lyceum and the Academy that the community of Christ was assembled, says Jerome, but from the lowest (*de vili plebecula*) in society. Christian writers expressly state that the new faith had only isolated adherents among the upper classes until the middle of the third century. Eusebius says that the peace the church enjoyed under Commodus (180 to 192) had helped a great deal to extend it, 'so that even many men in Rome prominent in wealth and birth turned to salvation with their whole household and clan'. Under Alexander Severus (222 to 235) Origen said that now the rich too, and even haughty and nobly-born ladies accepted the Christian message of the Word: successes therefore that Christianity could not claim previously. . . . From the time of Commodus on therefore the spread of Christianity in the upper orders is confirmed just as expressly and often as such testimony is lacking for the earlier period. . . . The only people of high rank in the period before Commodus whose conversion to Christianity is conceded as being very probable are Flavius Clemens, consul, executed in 95, and Flavia Domitilla, his wife or sister, banished to Pontia.

This proletarian character is one of the principal reasons for our being so ill-informed about the beginnings of Christianity. Its first champions may have been eloquent orators, but they were not expert in reading and writing. Those were arts that were even further removed from the masses of the people than they are today. For generations the Christian doctrine and the history of its communities were confined to oral traditions, traditions handed down by people who were feverishly excited and incredibly credulous, traditions dealing with events in which only a small group were involved, in so far as they took place at all; and hence traditions that could not be tested by the mass of the people, and especially by its critical, impartial elements. The putting down of these traditions in writing began only as better educated elements, of higher social standing, began to turn towards Christianity, and then this recording had a polemical not a historical purpose; it aimed at supporting definite views and demands.

It requires a great deal of boldness, as well as of bias, in addition to total ignorance of the conditions of historical trustworthiness, to use documents that came into existence in this way and teem with impossibilities and crass contradictions, to narrate the lives of individuals and even their speeches, in detail. We showed at the outset that it is impossible to make any concrete statement about the alleged founder of the Christian community. On the basis of what has been said thus far, we can add that there is no need to know anything concrete about him. All the systems of ideas that are usually indicated as characterizing Christianity, whether in praise or in blame, have been seen to be products of the Greco-Roman or the Judaic development. There is not a single Christian thought that would make it necessary to refer to some sublime prophet and superman, no thought that can not be traced in the 'heathen' or Jewish literature.

But although it is of no significance for our historical insight to be instructed as to the personalities of Jesus and his disciples, it is of the utmost importance to be clear about the character of the primitive Christian community. [pp. 274-5]

The Acts of the Apostles nowhere states that the apostles first organized the community after the death of Jesus; we find it already organized at that time, holding meetings of its members and performing its functions. The first mention of communism in *The Acts of the Apostles* runs as follows: 'And they continued steadfastly in the apostles' doctrine and fellowship, and in breaking of bread, and in prayers' (2, verse 42). That is, they continued their previous common meals and other communistic practices. If this had been newly introduced after the death of Jesus, the version would have to be quite different.

The communal organization was the link that kept Jesus' following together even after his death and preserved the memory of their crucified champion, who had proclaimed himself to be the Messiah, according to the tradition. The more the organization grew, and the more powerful it became, the more its martyrs must have occupied the imagination of the members, and the more they must have revolted at considering the crucified Messiah as false; the more too must they have felt themselves impelled to regard him as the genuine one, despite his death, as the Messiah that would come again in all his glory; the more they inclined to believe in his resurrection, and the more did faith in the Messianic nature of the crucified one and in his resurrection become the mark of the organization, setting it apart from the believers in other Messiahs. If the belief in the resurrection of the crucified Messiah had grown out of personal impression, it must have grown weaker and weaker with the passing of time, and tended to be replaced by other impressions, and finally disappeared with those who had known Jesus personally. But if the belief in the resurrection of him who was crucified stemmed from the effect that his organization produced, that belief would become stronger and more luxuriant as the organization grew; and the less positive information there was about the person of Jesus, the less the imagination of his worshippers would be hampered by definite facts.

It was not belief in the resurrection of him who was crucified that created the Christian community and lent it strength, but the converse: the vitality of the community created the belief in the continued life of their Messiah. [pp. 322–3]

As we have seen, the apostles were pushed into the background by the prophets in the second century. Both however, apostles as well as prophets, could often clash with the bishop, who would not hesitate to make his financial and moral power felt. It would not be hard for him to make life in the community miserable for apostles and prophets, and teachers too, if any of them manifested tendencies he did not care for. And that would happen frequently enough, especially with apostles and prophets.

Bishops, that is men who dealt with money, would not be chosen from among unworldly enthusiasts, but rather sober, business-like practical men. These men knew how to appreciate the value of money and of prosperous moneyed members of the community. It would be they who would represent opportunistic revisionism in the Christian community and work to mitigate hatred against the rich within it, to tone down the doctrines of the community in a way that would make it pleasanter for wealthy people to remain within it. . . .

Thus the bishop became the centre both of the economic and propaganda work of the community; in this case too ideology had to give way to economics.

There now grew up an official doctrine, recognized and propagated by the bureacracy of the community; views that differed from it were put down by all the means at their disposal. [pp. 380–1]

Thus the organization of a proletarian subversive communism gave rise to the most faithful support of despotism and exploitation, a source of new despotism, of new exploitation. The victorious Church congregation was at every point the precise opposite of that congregation which had been founded three centuries before by poor Galilean fishermen and peasants and Jerusalem proletarians. . . . [p. 448]

While the monastic system in its beginnings imparted new life to the communistic enthusiasm in Christianity it nevertheless finally took the same path that the clergy of the Church had taken before it. Like the clergy, it became an organisation for exploitation and domination. [p. 456]

Foundations of Christianity, trans. Henry F. Mins, Russell, N.Y. 1953.

Against all this can be stressed the essentially religious nature of the community. It can be argued that neither Jesus nor the Church which followed him was at all concerned with social reform. Their expectation of the coming of the Kingdom made social and economic aspirations of little relevance. All social policies could only be interim ones awaiting 'the day of the Lord'. Out of this other-worldy attitude came an indifference to the affairs of society, which characterized the message of Jesus, and eventually definite hostility to the world. This hostility was to be increased by monastic asceticism with its flight from secular life. The Church was certainly a well-defined social organization, but her social action was concerned with those within her fold. Her organisation was to influence secular life in the civilization of the Middle Ages, but in the pagan Empire the Christian communities stood apart from the society about them, a state within a state.

Some have indeed emphasized that the total ideal of Christianity was asceticism, that it had no ambition to infuse into the secular callings its ideals of trust in God and love of neighbour. It did not seek to include society in its inner ideal, did not seek to involve political life, social life, the economic order and the forces like science and art which inform human civilization.

Christianity, on this view, began as a detachment from social conditions and aspirations. In this it contrasted strongly with Stoicism, whose devotees, being upper class, did not think of detaching themselves from their possessions or status or office.

The early Church, it seems, never became totally altruistic in the sense of ministering to the greater alien community round about it. Its love was a 'love of the brethren'. The outer community was seen as a hostile 'city of the world'. Christians did not aim to keep that city going. They were unconcerned about the defence of frontiers, and until a late date were reluctant to serve in the Roman army, for they considered the 'warfare of Christ' to be the only campaign necessary. They were generally undisturbed about maintaining traditional culture; at best, selected parts of that culture could be borrowed to support their own gospel. This aloofness was obviously a first hint of conflict between Church and State, and perhaps of ultimate estrangement of the Church from society.

This means that the historian cannot adequately describe either religion or philosophy entirely in terms of social movement. Though pagan philosophy produced many ideas, for instance Zeno's 'society of humanity', which could have inspired social change, and though the cultivated criticism of philosophers must have been politically influential, there is no evidence that such ideas were based on class movements for social freedom. The spiritualization of pagan philosophy had not been the result of any social campaign. As for Christianity, even in Pliny's day there were already Christians from all classes (omnis ordinis). The social condition of Christians changed as more and more upper-class converts came in, and when we reach the fourth century the change is very noticeable. The later Christian literature puts us constantly in touch with the mannered refinement of the educated classes: with Marcella in her stately home on the Aventine, with the professors Libanius and Donatus, with Ausonius on his Gallic estates, with the asceticism of the cultured senator, Paulinus of Nola. Some Christians, like Prohaeresius, were actually professors of philosophy, but the crisis of conscience which such a post might involve is seen in Augustine's decision to abandon his professorial chair when he was baptized. There is tension between the faith and the society around it.

Historians, then, who assert a cultural or religious a priori will not be satisfied with an explanation that limits itself to social and economic factors.

3 ERNST TROELTSCH

It is, therefore, clear that the rise of Christianity is a religious and not a social phenomenon. For although religion is interwoven with life as a whole, in development and dialectic it has an independent existence. A new era of creative religious experience and sensitiveness to religious influences characterized the close of the ancient world. The way had been prepared for this change by a number of factors, which may be briefly enumerated: the destruction of national religions, which was a natural result of the loss of national independence; the mingling of races, which led naturally to the mingling of various cults; the rise of mystery-religions, with their exclusive emphasis upon the inward life, and their independence of questions of nationality and birth; the fusion of various fragments of religion which had broken away from their national foundation; the philosophical religion of culture with its varied forms of assimilation to the popular religions; the need of a world empire for a world religion, a need which was only partially satisfied by worship of the Emperor; the amazing deepening and spiritualizing of ethical thought during a period of intellectual development which covered four hundred years of unexampled richness in criticism and intensive growth; and, finally, the decline of polytheism (which was connected with all these factors) both in its *Mythus* and in its form of worship, and the desire for a final form of religion which would offer eternal values to mankind.

The close of the era of antiquity was marked by two outstanding developments: (*a*) the destruction of the popular religions, due to a variety of causes, though in the last resort it was due to the fact that religious thought itself had gradually become more spiritual and more ethical; (*b*) a new and powerful religious movement, due to the mingling of many varied currents of thought. Ultimately, however, this development was the result of an independent development in the religious idea itself. It was out of this situation that Christianity arose; the Church became the receptacle for the new ideas which grew out of this religious development, and, as far as possible, it linked them up with the fundamental doctrines of Christianity.

If, however, the process which I have just described gives a true picture of the relation of Christianity to the inner religious development of the ancient world, we see at once the reason for its appeal to the lower classes, and its development from them. This attitude, however, cannot be explained as the alleged product of a social process, but simply as one which has arisen out of the nature of a new religious movement. New religious movements of this kind develop along two lines; on the one hand, they proceed from the rarefied atmosphere of cultivated thoughtful circles, and express themselves in criticism and speculation; their actual importance depends upon the depth of the real religious vitality which these forms of criticism and speculation conceal. Platonism and Stoicism, each in its own way, are examples of new religious movements of this kind. Essentially, however, both are systems of reflection and attempts to reach truth through the reason, and therefore they never achieve the specifically religious power of a faith founded on revelation. Conscious of their weakness, they cling in part to the old popular religion, which they merely explain in somewhat different terms, and in part they base their confidence on the power of the abstract arguments which each individual may construct for himself after quiet reflection on the explanations offered by these systems. On the other hand, it is the lower classes which do the really creative work, forming communities on a genuine religious basis. They alone unite imagination and simplicity of feeling with a non-reflective habit of mind, a primitive energy, and an urgent sense of need. On such a foundation alone is it possible to build up an unconditional authoritative faith in a Divine Revelation with simplicity of surrender and unshaken certainty. Only within a fellowship of this kind is there room for those who have a sense of spiritual need, and who have not acquired the habit of intellectual reasoning, which always regards everything from a relative point of view. All great religious movements based on Divine revelation which have created large communities have always issued from circles of this kind. The meaning and capacity for development of the religious movement which arose in this way were always dependent upon the power and depth of the stimulus which had been imparted by such a naïve revelation, and, on the other hand, upon the energy of the religious conviction which gave to this stimulus a divine and absolute authority. Of course, it cannot be claimed that such movements are always characterized by a deep inward energy. But where this *is* the case simplicity is manifestly superior to speculation, for it produces a driving force and imparts a deep spiritual experience without which no religious movement can live. Inevitably, as the movement develops, the early naïve vital religious content always fuses with all the highest religious forces of the intellectual culture of the day; apart from this fusion faith would be broken by the impact of the cultural environment.

From the second century onwards this kind of fusion took place in the history of Christianity. The fact that the connection between faith and thought increased as time went on was a sure sign that the new faith contained a deep religious power; which not only did not break down when it came into touch with intellectual culture, but rather became more fruitful and developed still further. The Christian origins, however, reveal the popular character and outlook of all naïve religion. This is the reason why the new faith bore no trace of the much-discussed 'senility' of the Imperial period. Jesus Himself was a man of the people, and His Gospel bears clear traces of the simple peasant and artisan conditions of Galilee. It is only the poor and the humble who easily understand His Gospel; it is difficult for the rich and for the religious leaders because they do not feel their need. In their wisdom they cannot see the wood for the trees, and their hearts are attached to too many other things to be able to offer an unconditional surrender; yet 'with God all things are possible'; even a rich man can be saved, and even a scribe may not be far from the Kingdom of God.

Another quite obvious point, which was very important, is this: a religion which sets its adherents in absolute opposition to the State religion, and to the social and civic customs with which it is connected, can only now and again, quite exceptionally, win its adherents among those circles which, by their wealth and education, are most closely connected with these institutions. It was for the same reason that the Austrian *Los-von-Rom* movement, for example, was most successful among the lower classes; they were less closely bound up with the dominant religious system. In so far as this was the case, it is obvious that the religious movement was strongly, though indirectly, influenced by the social situation. The religious community has to do something for its members beyond the mere preaching of salvation; it has to try to provide men with shelter and assistance during the period of their earthly struggle. Thus the influence of the social situation becomes direct as soon as the Christian community is able to give help on these lines. But the more the Christian community becomes a society within a society, or a state within the State, the more strongly it becomes conscious of the fact that it is bound up with concrete social problems, and it then turns its attention and its power of organization to these matters. All this, however, is simply the result of the new religious idea, it is not its starting-point.

If this is so, however, it is a great mistake to treat all the ideas which underlie the preaching of Jesus as though they were primarily connected with the 'Social' problem. The message of Jesus is obviously purely religious; it issues directly from a very definite idea of God, and of the Divine Will in relation to man. To Jesus the whole meaning of life is religious; His life and His teaching are wholly determined by His thought of God. At the same time we must also remember that late Judaism shared the prevalent religious tendency of the ancient world; that is to say, here also politics and social disintegration had shaken men's faith in finite ideals, and had caused them to look with longing towards the horizon of the infinite. Once this is realized, however, it is quite permissible to study the connection between the sociological problem and these religious ideals; we may then inquire how the relation between the individual and Society in general is shaped from this religious standpoint, and how the sociological result which follows every fresh revelation of truth is affected by this religious idea. This certainly brings us up sharply against some very important points; it is essential to note that their peculiar significance is due precisely to the fact that they have been produced by the religious idea.

The Social Teaching of the Christian Churches, 1912; Eng. trans. London 1931, vol. i, pp. 43–5, 50–1

An historian whose prime interest is religion will be likely to welcome this emphasis on religious factors independent of economics and social trends. But he may still want to assess the effect of the alien Greek culture on Christian faith. And he might decide that the effect was a bad one. He might conclude that the Hellenist development was a deviation from the original Jewish intention of Jesus. This problem of 'Jesus and the Church', as we have seen, has divided historical opinion, though Christian historians generally assert that the Church's doctrine, whatever Hellenic garb it came to assume, remained true to its original insights.

Some have nevertheless maintained that philosophy adulterated the essential emphasis of the Christian religion. To take one example, the original religious sense of the word 'faith' (pistis) as the human trust in divine fatherhood, or the trust of the paralytic in the healing power of Jesus, finally came to mean mental assent to, and ability to recite, correct credal formulae; it might be argued, then, that the Christian emphasis had changed from a practical ethic into a debased intellectualism. It is interesting to find the heretic Eunomius chiding the orthodox Saint Basil for quoting the intellectual wisdom of the pagans when he should be quoting the laws of God. Gregory of Nyssa, who writes the defence of Basil, is himself so philosophic that the reader is amazed at the number of abstractions he can use to talk about human events. This is a far cry from the primitive Christian simplicity and has been viewed by some historians as a distortion of it.

4 EDWIN HATCH

Christianity came into a ground which was already prepared for it. Education was widely diffused over the Greek world, and among all classes of the community. It had not merely aroused the habit of inquiry which is the foundation of philosophy, but had also taught certain philosophical methods. Certain elements of the philosophical temper had come into existence on a large scale, penetrating all classes of society and inwrought into the general intellectual fibre of the time. They had produced a certain habit of mind. When, through the kinship of ideas, Christianity had been absorbed by the educated classes, the habit of mind which had preceded it remained and dominated. It showed itself mainly in three ways:

1. The first of these was the tendency to define. The earliest Christians had been content to believe in God and to worship Him, without endeavouring to define precisely the conception of Him which lay beneath their faith and their worship. They looked up to Him as their Father in heaven. They thought of Him as one, as beneficent, and as supreme. But they drew no fence of words round their idea of Him, and still less did they attempt to demonstrate by processes of reason that their idea of Him was true. But there is an anecdote quoted with approval by Eusebius from Rhodon, a controversialist of the latter part of the second century, which furnishes a striking proof of the growing strength at that time of the philosophical temper. It relates the main points of a short controversy between Rhodon and Apelles. Apelles was in some respects in sympathy with Marcion, and in some respects followed the older Christian tradition. He refused to be drawn into the new philosophizing current; and Rhodon attacked him for his conservatism. 'He was often refuted for his errors, which indeed made him say that we ought not to inquire too closely into doctrine; but that as every one had believed, so he should remain. For he declared that those who set their hopes on the Crucified One would be saved, if only they were found in good works. But the most uncertain thing of all that he said was what he said about God. He held no doubt that there is One Principle, just as we hold too: but when I said to him, "Tell us how you demonstrate that, or on what grounds you are able to assert that there is One Principle," ... he said that he did not know, but that that was his conviction. When I thereupon adjured him to tell the truth, he swore that he was telling the truth, that he did not know

how there is one unbegotten God, but that nevertheless so he believed. Then I laughed at him and denounced him, for that, giving himself out to be a teacher, he did not know how to prove what he taught.'

2. The second manifestation of the philosophical habit of mind was the tendency to speculate, that is, to draw inferences from definitions, to weave the inferences into systems, and to test assertions by their logical consistency or inconsistency with those systems. The earliest Christians had but little conception of a system. The inconsistency of one apparently true statement with another did not vex their souls. Their beliefs reflected the variety of the world and of men's thoughts about the world. It was one of the secrets of the first great successes of Christianity. There were different and apparently irreconcilable elements in it. It appealed to men of various mould. It furnished a basis for the construction of strangely diverse edifices. But the result of the ascendency of philosophy was, that in the fourth and fifth centuries the majority of churches insisted not only upon a unity of belief in the fundamental facts of Christianity, but also upon a uniformity of speculations in regard to those facts. The premises of those speculations were assumed; the conclusions logically followed: the propositions which were contrary or contradictory to them were measured, not by the greater or less probability of the premises, but by the logical certainty of the conclusions; and symmetry became a test of truth.

3. The new habit of mind manifested itself not less in the importance which came to be attached to it. The holding of approved opinions was elevated to a position at first co-ordinate with, and at last superior to, trust in God and the effort to live a holy life. There had been indeed from the first an element of knowledge in the conception of the means of salvation. The knowledge of the facts of the life of Jesus Christ necessarily precedes faith in him. But under the touch of Greek philosophy, knowledge had become speculation: whatever obligation attached to faith in its original sense was conceived to attach to it in its new sense: the new form of knowledge was held to be not less necessary than the old.

The Western communities not only took over the greater part of the inheritance, but also proceeded to assume in a still greater degree the correspondence of ideas with realities, and of inferences about ideas with truth about realities. It added such large groups to the sum of them, that in the dogmatic theology of Latin and Teutonic Christendom the content is more Western than Eastern. But the conception of such a theology and its underlying assumptions are Greek. They come from the Greek tendency to attach the same certainty to meta-physical as to physical ideas. They are in reality built upon a quicksand. There is no more reason to suppose that God has revealed metaphysics than that He has revealed chemistry. The Christian revelation is, at least primarily, a setting forth of certain facts. It does not in itself afford a guarantee of the certainty of the speculations which are built upon those facts. All such speculations are *dogmas* in the original sense of the word. They are simply personal convictions. To the statement of one man's convictions other men may assent: but they can never be quite sure that they understand its terms in the precise sense in which the original framer of the statement understood them.

The belief that metaphysical theology is more than this, is the chief bequest of Greece to religious thought, and it has been a *damnosa hereditas*. It has given to later Christianity that part of it which is doomed to perish, and which yet, while it lives, holds the key of the prison-house of many souls.

The Influence of Greek Ideas on the Christian Church, London 1888; New York, Harper 1957, pp. 134–8

On the other hand it is difficult to see how Christianity could ever have made its missionary way in the Hellenic world without turning philosophic. Even Paul seemed to be aware of this when he addressed an Athenian audience, for he suddenly put aside Rabbinical style and adopted a more philosophic idiom; indeed he seems to have attempted to put over an image of himself as a new Socrates 'importing new gods'. The Greeks would not take to a religion which was all a matter of practical conduct, with no intellectual content, no gnosis. On the Greek scene, therefore, speculative dogma was inevitable. Only a rare voice, and not a Greek one, cried that the Christian religion was different from mere intellectual vision, or that 'God did not covenant to save his flock by dialectic.' The Greeks were culture-minded, and so Greek Christian writers gradually came to view their faith as a culture and not as an opponent of culture. In this attitude European man remained Hellenist; when the revival of Greek study came at the Renaissance the greatest of the humanists expressed his cultural ideal as a philosophia Christi. *The Christian thinkers could not gainsay Aristotle's notion that culture represented a need of man's nature, and therefore, they argued, it was willed by man's Creator. Accordingly they sought to combine their religion with existing humanism, and to think of it, in fact, as a combination of the 'study of God' with the 'study of* man' (philanthropia), *which sounds a remarkably Hellenic version of the Rabbinical precept of Jesus to love God and love neighbour; one understands why historians like Harnack and Hatch view the transition with disfavour.*

The historian whose prime interest is not the progress or decline of Christianity but the rise of European humanism and science may have another sort of complaint. He may indeed view the rise of Christianity as the very death of ancient rationalism and of the whole civilization which nourished it. He might decide, having followed the course of Greek thought from its cradle of Ionic speculation to its final submission to the Church's theology, that the result was a set-back for civilization. If he took rational philosophy to be the most impressive achievement of the Greek mind, with its perennial human problems written down in shapely prose, his lament would be that this achievement was surrendered to a popular religious movement which entered Hellenism from the East, by the victory of exotic emotionalism over intellect:

> The Babylonian starlight brought
> A fabulous formless darkness in;
> Odour of blood when Christ was slain
> Made all Platonic tolerance vain
> And vain all Doric discipline. (W. B. YEATS)

Gibbon, for instance, finding here, as in all history, 'little more than the register of the crimes, follies and misfortunes of mankind', views the transition from ancient philosopher to Christian monk as the epitome of 'decline and fall' in the ancient civilization.

5 EDWARD GIBBON

The monastic saints, who excite only the contempt and pity of a philosopher, were respected and almost adored by the prince and people. Successive crowds of pilgrims from Gaul and India saluted the divine pillar of Simeon; the tribes of Saracens disputed in arms the honour of his benediction; the queens of Arabia and Persia gratefully confessed his supernatural virtue; and the angelic Hermit was consulted by the younger Theodosius in the most important concerns of the church and state. His remains were transported from the mountains of Telenissa, by a solemn procession of the patriarch, the master-general of the East, six bishops, twenty-one counts or tribunes, and six thousand soldiers; and Antioch revered his bones as her glorious ornament and impregnable defence. The fame of the apostles and martyrs was gradually eclipsed by these recent and popular Anachorets; the Christian world fell prostrate before their shrines; and the miracles ascribed to their relics exceeded, at least in number and duration, the spiritual exploits of their lives. But the golden legend of their lives was embellished by the artful credulity of their interested brethren; and a believing age was easily persuaded that the slightest caprice of an Egyptian or a Syrian monk had been sufficient to interrupt the eternal laws of the universe. The favourites of Heaven were accustomed to cure inveterate diseases with a touch, a word, or a distant message; and to expel the most obstinate demons from the souls or bodies which they possessed. They familiarly accosted, or imperiously commanded, the lions and serpents of the desert; infused vegetation into a sapless trunk; suspended iron on the surface of the water; passed the Nile on the back of a crocodile; and refreshed themselves in a fiery furnace. These extravagant tales, which display the fiction, without the genius, of poetry, have seriously affected the reason, the faith, and the morals of the Christians. Their credulity debased and vitiated the faculties of the mind: they corrupted the evidence of history; and superstition gradually extinguished the hostile light of philosophy and science. Every mode of religious worship which had been practised by the saints, every mysterious doctrine which they believed, was fortified by the sanction of divine revelation, and all the manly virtues were oppressed by the servile and pusillanimous reign of the monks. If it be possible to measure the interval between the philosophic writings of Cicero and the sacred legend of Theodoret, between the character of Cato and that of Simeon, we may appreciate the memorable revolution which was accomplished in the Roman empire within a period of five hundred years.

Decline and Fall of the Roman Empire, London, 1776–88, ch. 37

Similarly, a famous historian of Greek philosophy when he pauses at the end of his work to survey the whole story is equally depressed by the final exhaustion of Greek rationalism.

6 EDUARD ZELLER

Boldly, almost impetuously, Greek philosophy had in the sixth century B.C. trod the way which leads from myth to the Logos. Trusting in the power of the human mind, the great pre-Socratic Ionians, Plato and Aristotle built up their systems on a basis of science and superseded the mythical ideas. Socrates, the minor schools which took their rise from him, and the Hellenistic philosophy of the Stoa and Epicureanism were all united in maintaining that ethical conduct of man depends on his knowledge. This intellectualism that proclaimed the autonomy of human reason formed the backbone in the organic development of Greek philosophy. But at an early date this rationalistic tendency was crossed by a religious influence which originated in the last instance in the East. This was Orphicism, which with its separation of body and soul, matter and mind, god and the world, grafted dualism upon Greek thought and relied on divine revelations instead of rational proof. The Greek mind in men like Pythagoras and his pupils, Empedocles and Plato, endeavoured to comprehend this doctrine and elaborate it on rational grounds. But it remained something foreign in Greek intellectual life. In the Hellenistic period and the Roman Empire, when not only the orient was hellenized but the Greek world, too, was to a large extent orientalized, this tendency received fresh support and strength from its old home. Posidonius exhibits in a higher degree the tendency, which had always been strong in the Stoa, to reconcile philosophy and religion. Now the power of philosophic speculation which had been weakened by scepticism showed itself in neo-Pythagoreanism, the Hellenistic–Jewish philosophy and in neo-Platonism as no longer strong enough to dam the stream of religious mysticism which was now sweeping in full force into philosophy. However much we may admire the last revival of antique thought in the philosophic system of Plotinus, it nevertheless bears the stamp of a non-Greek nature and traces of decadence which became more numerous and more pronounced in his successors. In the hands of Iamblichus and Proclus philosophy was petrified into scholasticism, the characteristic of which is that it no longer sought to supersede mythical ideas by empirical research and independent rational thought, but saw its task in supporting the traditional religion with reason and in presenting it as intellectually comprehensible. Here knowledge is replaced by revelation in ecstasy. After Greek philosophy had performed this self-castration it sank exhausted into the arms of religion; as Proclus expresses in one of his hymns to the gods:

'And so let me anchor, weary one, in the haven of piety.'

This development was completed both in epistemology and metaphysics, ethics and politics. Here, too, Orphicism had familiarized the

Greeks with an asceticism which was wholly contrary to their nature and in connection with the idea of salvation, the saving of the soul. That is the exact opposite of the Socratic *autarkeia* based on knowledge. The Greek was also familiar with the repression or limitation of natural bodily needs, but only from the point of view of endurance which was aimed at increasing the control and capacity of the body. On the other hand the Orphic asceticism, which was revived in neo-Pythagoreanism and neo-Platonism, served religious and cathartic ends, the liberation of the soul from the supposed impurity of the body. It finally absorbed the Cynical form of asceticism, which was aimed originally at ensuring the independence of the individual, and passed over with it into the Christian monasticism (Aug. *Civ. Dei*, XIX, 19). In the Aristotelean philosophy and especially in its last phase, Neoplatonism, asceticism was accompanied by the recedence of political ideas and the growth of individualism in philosophy which had been initiated by Cynicism and furthered by Epicureanism. This found further support in the fact that not only the Greek Polis but also all ancient states had been absorbed into the Roman Empire. The Stoic thought of a world-state comprising all men lived on in the form of the Christian world-church uniting all in one faith for the salvation of the soul.

Outlines of the History of Greek Philosophy, trans. L. K. Palmer, Kegan Paul, 1931, pp. 313–15

And the most renowned English Hellenist of the twentieth century having traced the impressive history of ancient Greek literature ends by lamenting that 'twilight of the gods' in which the rational ideals first cultivated by the Greeks, the ideals of freedom, of beauty, and of reason, withered and died.

7 GILBERT MURRAY

Götterdämmerung

Longus . . . is the last man, unless the present writer's knowledge is at fault, who lives for mere Beauty with the old whole-hearted devotion, as Plotînus lived for speculative Truth, as Julian for the 'great city of gods and men'. Of these three ideals, to which, beyond all others, Greece had opened the eyes of mankind, that of Political Freedom and Justice had long been relegated from practical life to the realm of thought, and those who had power paid no heed to it. The search for

Truth was finally made hopeless when the world, mistrusting Reason, weary of argument and wonder, flung itself passionately under the spell of a system of authoritative Revelation, which acknowledged no truth outside itself, and stamped free inquiry as sin. And who was to preach the old Beauty, earnest and frank and innocent, to generations which had long ceased to see it or to care for it? The intellect of Greece died ultimately of that long discouragement which works upon nations like slow poison. She ceased to do her mission because her mission had ceased to bear fruit. And the last great pagans, men like Plotînus, Longus and Julian, pronounce their own doom and plead for their own pardon, when they refuse to strike new notes or to try the ring of their own voices, content to rouse mere echoes of that old call to Truth, to Beauty, to Political Freedom and Justice, with which Greece had awakened the world long ago, when the morning was before her, and her wings were strong.

A History of Ancient Greek Literature, London, 1897, pp. 404–5

Perhaps, of course, Platonic rationalism was overdone in both Greek thought and Christianity. The argument has been advanced that speculative philosophy was a decline from the true spirit of Greek science, and even from Greek tragedy, where human instinct nourished by religious initiation had held rational factors in balance. By adopting Platonic idealism Christianity became a denial of life, opposing everything empirical, instinctive, vital, prophetic, in European man; its doctrine relying on 'supernatural' dogmatism more than on intuitive awareness or poetry; its society based on the 'herd', 'the humble of heart', to the exclusion of personal initiative and power. From such polemic, pioneered by Nietzsche, many modern writers have accepted that 'God is dead' and that the cosmos is 'absurd'.

Nietzsche's fiery eye saw in Christianity the triumph of an anti-Hellene, anti-Epicurean, anti-scientific spirit, which cunningly adopted Platonic idealism with its nebulous and fascinating dogmatism about the superhuman, a spirituality that was to be the death of factual science, and of all natural instinct and taste and energy. But Europe had, he thought, sporadically struggled against this dogmatism which affected blindness to the natural imperfections and inequalities of men and established a ghetto culture of the common herd. The early Christians arbitrarily distorted their Master's teaching to develop their mob religion, a religion of the weakling and the pessimist, of the ambiguous unscientific mind, of the antihuman.

Between the lines of Nietzsche's history the reader senses his disturbing tenet that nature has divided off mankind clearly into two classes, supermen and slaves, Christianity being of the latter. A controlling assumption of safer proportions might have been that there is something of ruler and something of slave in everybody.

8 FRIEDRICH W. NIETZSCHE

Many educated people still believe that the triumph of Christianity over Greek philosophy is a proof of the greater truthfulness of the former – although in this case it is only the coarser and more powerful that has triumphed over the more spiritual and delicate. Which possesses the greater truth may be seen from the fact that the awakening sciences have agreed with Epicurus' philosophy on point after point, but on point after point have rejected Christianity.

Human, All–Too–Human, trans. Helen Zimmern, London, Foulis, 1910, p. 80

For heaven's sake, do not throw Plato at me. I am a complete sceptic about Plato, and I have never been able to join in the admiration for the *artist* Plato which is customary among scholars. In the end, the subtlest judges of taste among the ancients themselves are here on my side. Plato, it seems to me, throws all stylistic forms together and is thus a first-rate decadent in style: his responsibility is thus comparable to that of the Cynics, who invented the *satura Menippea*. To be attracted by the Platonic dialogue, this horribly self-satisfied and childish kind of dialectic, one must never have read good French writers – Fontenelle, for example. Plato is boring. In the end, my mistrust of Plato goes deep: he represents such an aberration from all the basic instincts of the Hellene, is so moralistic, so pre-existently Christian – he already takes the concept 'good' for the highest concept – that for the whole phenomenon Plato I would sooner use the harsh phrase, 'higher swindle', or, if it sounds better, 'idealism,' than any other. We have paid dearly for the fact that this Athenian got his schooling from the Egyptians (or from the Jews in Egypt?). In that great calamity, Christianity, Plato represents that ambiguity and fascination, called an 'ideal', which made it possible for the nobler spirits of antiquity to misunderstand themselves and to set foot on the bridge leading to the cross. And how much

Plato there still is in the concept 'church', in the construction, system, and practice of the church!

Twilight of the Idols, ed. W. A. Kaufmann, *The Portable Nietzsche*, N.Y., Viking Press, 1954, p. 557

The philosophy of the dogmatists, it is to be hoped, was only a promise for thousands of years afterwards, as was astrology in still earlier times, in the service of which probably more labour, gold, acuteness, and patience have been spent than on any actual science hitherto: we owe to it, and to its 'super-terrestrial' pretensions in Asia and Egypt, the grand style of architecture. It seems that in order to inscribe themselves upon the heart of humanity with everlasting claims, all great things have first to wander about the earth as enormous and awe-inspiring caricatures: dogmatic philosophy has been a caricature of this kind – for instance, the Vedanta doctrine in Asia, and Platonism in Europe. Let us not be ungrateful to it, although it must certainly be confessed that the worst, the most tiresome, and the most dangerous of errors hitherto has been a dogmatist error – namely, Plato's invention of Pure Spirit and the Good in Itself. But now when it has been surmounted, when Europe, rid of this nightmare, can again draw breath freely and at least enjoy a healthier – sleep, we, *whose duty is wakefulness itself*, are the heirs of all the strength which the struggle against this error has fostered. It amounted to the very inversion of truth, and the denial of the *perspective* – the fundamental condition – of life, to speak of Spirit and the Good as Plato spoke of them; indeed one might ask, as a physician: 'How did such a malady attack that finest product of antiquity, Plato? Had the wicked Socrates really corrupted him? Was Socrates after all a corrupter of youths, and deserved his hemlock?' But the struggle against Plato, or – to speak plainer, and for the 'people' – the struggle against the ecclesiastical oppression of millenniums of Christianity (for Christianity is Platonism for the 'people'), produced in Europe a magnificent tension of soul, such as had not existed anywhere previously; with such a tensely-strained bow one can now aim at the furthest goals. As a matter of fact, the European feels this tension as a state of distress, and twice attempts have been made in grand style to unbend the bow: once by means of Jesuitism, and the second time by means of democratic enlightenment – which, with the aid of liberty of the press and newspaper-reading, might, in fact, bring it about that the spirit would not so easily find itself in 'distress'! (The Germans invented gunpowder – all credit to them! but they again made things square – they invented printing.) But we, who are neither Jesuits, nor democrats, nor even sufficiently Germans, we *good Europeans*, and free, *very free spirits* – we have it still, all the distress of spirit and all the tension of its bow! And perhaps also the arrow, the duty, and, who knows? *the goal to aim at. . . .*

Beyond Good and Evil, trans. H. Zimmern, London, Foulis 1911, Preface, pp. 2–3

If one could observe the strangely painful, equally coarse and refined comedy of European Christianity with the derisive and impartial eye of an Epicurean god, I should think one would never cease marvelling and laughing; does it not actually seem that some single will has ruled over Europe for eighteen centuries in order to make a *sublime abortion* of man? He, however, who, with opposite requirements (no longer Epicurean) and with some divine hammer in his hand, could approach this almost voluntary degeneration and stunting of mankind, as exemplified in the European Christian (Pascal, for instance), would he not have to cry aloud with rage, pity, and horror: 'Oh, you bunglers, presumptuous pitiful bunglers, what have you done! Was that a work for your hands? How you have hacked and botched my finest stone! What have *you* presumed to do!' – I should say that Christianity has hitherto been the most portentous of presumptions. Men, not great enough, nor hard enough, to be entitled as artists to take part in fashioning *man*; men, not sufficiently strong and far-sighted to *allow*, with sublime self-constraint, the obvious law of the thousandfold failures and perishings to prevail; men, not sufficiently noble to see the radically different grades of rank and intervals of rank that separate man from man – *such* men, with their 'equality before God', have hitherto swayed the destiny of Europe; until at last a dwarfed, almost ludicrous species has been produced, a gregarious animal, something obliging, sickly, mediocre, the European of the present day.

Beyond Good and Evil, trans. H. Zimmern, London, Foulis, 1911, p. 84

The *Christians* have done exactly what the Jews did before them. They introduced what they conceived to be an innovation and a thing necessary to self-preservation into their Master's teaching, and wove His life into it. They likewise credited Him with all the wisdom of a maker of proverbs – *in short*, they represented their everyday life and activity as an act of obedience, and thus sanctioned their propaganda.

What it all depends upon, may be gathered from Paul: it is *not much*. What remains is the development of a type of saint, out of the values which these people regarded as saintly.

The whole of the 'doctrine of miracles', including the resurrection, is the result of self-glorification on the part of the community, which ascribed to its Master those qualities it ascribed to itself, but in a higher degree (or, better still, it derived its strength from Him. . . .).

Christianity has become something fundamentally different from what its Founder wished it to be. It is the great *anti-pagan movement* of antiquity, formulated with the use of the life, teaching, and 'words' of the Founder of Christianity, but interpreted quite *arbitrarily*, according to a scheme embodying *profoundly different needs*: translated into the language of all the *subterranean religions* then existing.

It is the rise of Pessimism (whereas Jesus wished to bring the peace and the happiness of the lambs): and moreover the Pessimism of the weak, of the inferior, of the suffering, and of the oppressed.

Its mortal enemies are (1) *Power*, whether in the form of character, intellect, or taste, and 'worldliness'; (2) the 'good cheer' of classical times, the noble levity and scepticism, hard pride, eccentric dissipation, and cold frugality of the sage, Greek refinement in manners, words, and form. Its mortal enemy is as much the *Roman* as the *Greek*.

The attempt on the part of *anti-paganism* to establish itself on a philosophical basis, and to make its tenets possible: it shows a taste for the ambiguous figures of ancient culture, and above all for Plato, who was, more than any other, an anti-Hellene and Semite in instinct. . . . It also shows a taste for Stoicism, which is essentially the work of Semites ('dignity' is regarded as severity, law; virtue is held to be greatness, self-responsibility, authority, greatest sovereignty over oneself – this is Semitic. The Stoic is an Arabian sheik wrapped in Greek togas and notions).

The Will to Power, trans. A. M. Ludovici, London, Foulis, 1910, pp. 157–9

The whole labour of the ancient world *in vain:* I have no word to express my feelings about something so tremendous. And considering that its labour was a preliminary labour, that only the foundation for the labours of thousands of years had just then been laid with granite self-confidence – the whole *meaning* of the ancient world in vain! Wherefore Greeks? Wherefore Romans?

All the presuppositions for a scholarly culture, all scientific *methods*, were already there; the great, the incomparable art of reading well had already been established – that presupposition for the tradition of culture, for the unity of science; natural science, allied with mathematics and mechanics, was well along on the best way – the *sense for facts*, the last and most valuable of all the senses, had its schools and its tradition of centuries. Is this understood? Everything *essential* had been found, so that the work could be begun: the methods, one must say it ten times, *are* what is essential, also what is most difficult, also what is for the longest time opposed by habits and laziness. What we today have again conquered with immeasurable self-mastery – for each of us still has the bad instincts, the Christian ones, in his system – the free eye before reality, the cautious hand, patience and seriousness in the smallest matters, the whole *integrity* in knowledge – that had already been there once before! More than two thousand years ago! *And*, in addition, the good, the delicate sense of tact and taste. *Not* as brain drill! *Not* as 'German' education with loutish manners! But as body, as gesture, as instinct – as reality, in short. *All in vain!* Overnight nothing but a memory.

Greeks! Romans! The nobility of instinct, the taste, the methodical research, the genius of organization and administration, the faith in, the *will* to, man's future, the great Yes to all things, become visible in the *imperium Romanum*, visible for all the senses, the grand style no longer mere art but become reality, truth, *life*. And not buried overnight by a natural catastrophe, not trampled down by Teutons and other buffaloes, but ruined by cunning, stealthy, invisible, anemic vampires. Not vanquished – merely drained. Hidden vengefulness, petty envy become master. Everything miserable that suffers from itself, that is afflicted with bad feelings, the whole ghetto-world of the soul *on top* all at once.

One need only read any Christian agitator, St Augustine, for example, to comprehend, to *smell*, what an unclean lot had thus come to the top. One would deceive oneself utterly if one presupposed any lack of intelligence among the leaders of the Christian movement: oh, they are clever, clever to the point of holiness, these good church fathers! What they lack is something quite different. Nature has neglected them – she forgot to give them a modest dowry of respectable, of decent, of *clean* instincts. Among ourselves, they are not even men. Islam is a thousand times right in despising Christianity: Islam presupposes *men*.

Twilight of the Idols, in *The Portable Nietzsche*, pp. 650–1

More recent history approaches Christian beginnings with less desire to categorize as bad or good. The moralizing approach was part of an old tradition. But modern history is less confined: it spreads out into philology, archaeology, comparative religion and psychology. It would be impossible, for instance, for a modern historian to be unaware of psychoanalysis. The psychologist sees religion as a 'psychic fact', a natural product of man's mental processes. Man invents out of his subconscious the myths that cheat mortality. The myth-making function is a biological urge, deep-seated and universal and primary. It is deeper than its historical manifestations. It is there before rational thought. 'The true has the false for its ancestor.' Fable is older than syllogism, and all religious attitudes and dogmas are its psychic product. God is very real to the psychologist, in the sense of being a psychic fact, a phenomenon in his subject.

The psychologist sees in the meeting of Greek rationalism and Christian faith something more than can be categorized superficially as 'decline and fall' or the reverse. He sees indeed the interplay of primordial conscious and unconscious forces in the life of humanity. He is not prepared to condemn religious dogma out of hand; its symbols may indeed appear to him as forces of integration in the psyche. He finds that certain such symbols have patterned the dreams of mankind over thousands of years and that they are much more powerful than purely rational habits of thought.

9 C. G. JUNG

In itself any scientific theory, no matter how subtle, has, I think, less value from the standpoint of psychological truth than religious dogma, for the simple reason that a theory is necessarily highly abstract and exclusively rational, whereas dogma expresses an irrational whole by means of imagery. This guarantees a far better rendering of an irrational fact like the psyche. Moreover, dogma owes its continued existence and its form on the one hand to so-called 'revealed' or immediate experiences of the 'Gnosis' – for instance, the God-man, the Cross, the Virgin Birth, the Immaculate Conception, the Trinity, and so on, and on the other hand to the ceaseless collaboration of many minds over many centuries. It may not be quite clear why I call certain dogmas 'immediate experiences', since in itself a dogma is the very thing that precludes immediate experience. Yet the Christian images I have mentioned are not peculiar to Christianity alone (although in Christianity they have undergone a development and intensification of meaning not to be found in any other religion). They occur just as often in pagan religions, and besides that they can reappear spontaneously in all sorts of variations as psychic phenomena, just as in the remote past they originated in visions, dreams, or trances. Ideas like these are never invented. They came into being before man had learned to use his mind purposively. Before man learned to produce thoughts, thoughts came to him. *He did not think – he perceived his mind functioning.* Dogma is like a dream, reflecting the spontaneous and autonomous activity of the objective psyche, the unconscious. Such an expression of the unconscious is a much more efficient means of defence against further immediate experiences than any scientific theory. The theory has to disregard the emotional values of the experience. The dogma, on the other hand, is extremely eloquent in just this respect. One scientific theory is soon superseded by another. Dogma lasts for untold centuries. The suffering God-Man may be at least five thousand years old and the Trinity is probably even older. [pp. 45–6]

The *quaternarium* or quaternity has a long history. It appears not only in Christian iconology and mystical speculation but plays perhaps a still greater role in Gnostic philosophy and from then on down through the Middle Ages until well into the eighteenth century. [p. 37]

I cannot refrain from calling attention to the interesting fact that whereas the central Christian symbolism is a Trinity, the formula presented by the unconscious is a quaternity. In reality the orthodox Christian formula is not quite complete, because the dogmatic aspect of the evil principle is absent from the Trinity and leads a more or less awkward existence on its own as the devil. Nevertheless it seems that the Church does not exclude an inner relationship between the devil and the Trinity. A Catholic authority expresses himself on this question as follows: 'The existence of Satan, however, can only be understood in relation to the Trinity.' 'Any theological treatment of the devil that is not related to God's trinitarian consciousness is a falsification of the actual position.' According to this view, the devil possesses personality and absolute freedom. That is why he can be the true, personal 'counterpart of Christ'. 'Herein is revealed a new freedom in God's being: he freely allows the devil to subsist beside him and permits his kingdom to endure for ever.' 'The idea of a mighty devil is incompatible with the conception of Yahweh, but not with the conception of the Trinity. The mystery of one God in Three Persons opens out a new freedom in the depths of God's being, and this even makes possible the thoughts of a personal devil existing alongside God and in opposition to him.' The devil, accordingly, possesses an autonomous personality, freedom, and eternality, and he has these metaphysical qualities so much in common with God that he can actually subsist in opposition to him. Hence the relationship or even the (negative) affinity of the devil with the Trinity can no longer be denied as a Catholic idea. [p. 59]

The *Timaeus*, which was the first to propound a triadic formula for the God-image in philosophical terms, starts off with the ominous question: 'One, two, three – but . . . where is the fourth?' This question is, as we know, taken up again in the Cabiri scene in *Faust*:

> *Three we brought with us,*
> *The fourth would not come.*
> *He was the right one*
> *Who thought for them all.*

When Goethe says that the fourth was the one 'who thought for them all', we rather suspect that the fourth was Goethe's own thinking function. The Cabiri are, in fact, the mysterious creative powers, the gnomes who work under the earth, i.e., below the threshold of consciousness, in order to supply us with lucky ideas. As imps and hob-goblins, however, they also play all sorts of nasty tricks, keeping back names and dates that were 'on the tip of the tongue', making us say the wrong thing, etc. They give an eye to everything that has not already been anticipated by the conscious mind and the functions at its disposal. As these functions can be used consciously only because they are adapted, it follows that the unconscious, autonomous function is not or cannot be used consciously because it is unadapted. The differentiated and differentiable functions are much easier to cope with, and, for under-standable reasons, we prefer to leave the 'inferior' function round the corner, or to repress it altogether, because it is such an awkward cus-tomer. And it is a fact that it has the strongest tendency to be infantile, banal, primitive, and archaic. Anybody who has a high opinion of himself will do well to guard against letting it make a fool of him. On the other hand, deeper insight will show that the primitive and archaic qualities of the inferior function conceal all sorts of significant relationships and symbolical meanings, and instead of laughing off the Cabiri as ridiculous Tom Thumbs he may begin to suspect that they are a treasure-house of hidden wisdom. Just as, in *Faust*, the fourth thinks for them all, so the whereabouts of the eighth should be asked 'on Olympus'. Goethe showed great insight in not underestimating his inferior function, thinking, although it was in the hands of the Cabiri and was undoubtedly mythological and archaic. He characterizes it perfectly in the line: 'The fourth would not come.' Exactly! It wanted for some reason to stay behind or below.

Three of the four orienting functions are available to consciousness. This is confirmed by the psychological experience that a rational type, for instance, whose superior function is thinking, has at his disposal one, or possibly two, auxiliary functions of an irrational nature, namely sensation (the 'fonction du réel') and intuition (perception via the unconscious). His inferior function will be feeling (valuation), which remains in a retarded state and is contaminated with the unconcious. It refuses to come along with the others and often goes wildly off on its own. This peculiar dissociation is, it seems, a product of civilization, and it denotes a freeing of consciousness from any excessive attachment to the 'spirit of gravity'. If that function, which is still bound indissolubly to the past and whose roots reach back as far as the animal kingdom, can be left behind and even forgotten, then consciousness has won for itself a new and not entirely illusory freedom. It can leap over abysses on winged feet; it can free itself from bondage to sense-impressions, emotions, fascinating thoughts, and presentiments by soaring into abstraction. Certain primitive initiations stress the idea of transformation into ghosts and invisible spirits and thereby testify to the relative emancipation of consciousness from the fetters of non-differentiation. Although there is a tendency, characteristic not only of primitive religions, to speak rather exaggeratedly of complete transformation, complete renewal and rebirth, it is, of course, only a relative change, continuity with the earlier state being in large measure preserved. Were it otherwise, every religious transformation would bring about a complete splitting of the personality or a loss of memory, which is obviously not so. The connection with the earlier attitude is maintained because part of the personality remains behind in the previous situation; that is to say it lapses into unconsciousness and starts building up the shadow. The loss makes itself felt in consciousness through the absence of at least one of the four orienting functions, and the missing function is always the opposite of the superior function. The loss need not necessarily take the form of complete absence; in other words, the inferior function may be either unconscious or conscious, but in both cases it is autonomous and obsessive and not influenceable by the will. It has the 'all-or-none' character of an instinct. Although emancipation from the instincts brings a differentiation and enhancement of consciousness, it can only come about at the expense of the unconscious function, so that conscious orientation lacks that element which the inferior function could have supplied. Thus it often happens that people who have an amazing range of consciousness know less about themselves than the veriest infant, and all because 'the fourth would not come' – it remained down below – or up above – in the unconscious realm.

As compared with the trinitarian thinking of Plato, ancient Greek philosophy favoured thinking of a quaternary type. In Pythagoras the great role was played not by three but by four; the Pythagorean oath, for instance, says that the tetraktys 'contains the roots of eternal nature'. The Pythagorean school was dominated by the idea that the soul was a square and not a triangle. The origin of these ideas lies far back in the dark prehistory of Greek thought. The quaternity is an archetype of almost universal occurrence. It forms the logical basis for any whole judgement. If one wishes to pass such a judgement, it must have this fourfold aspect. For instance, if you want to describe the horizon as a whole, you name the four quarters of heaven. Three is not a natural coefficient of order, but an artificial one. There are always four elements, four prime qualities, four colours, four castes, four ways of spiritual development, etc. So, too, there are four aspects of psychological orientation, beyond which nothing fundamental remains to be said. In order to orient ourselves, we must have a function which ascertains that something is there (sensation); a second function which establishes *what* it is (thinking); a third function which states whether it suits us or not, whether we wish to accept it or not (feeling); and a fourth function which indicates where it came from and where it is going (intuition). When this has been done, there is nothing more to say. Schopenhauer proves that the 'Principle of Sufficient Reason' has a fourfold root. This is so because the fourfold aspect is the minimum requirement for a complete judgement. The ideal of completeness is the circle or sphere, but its natural minimal division is a quaternity. [pp. 164–7]

Although it is extremely improbable that the Christian Trinity is

derived directly from the triadic World-Soul in the *Timaeus*, it is nevertheless rooted in the same archetype. If we wish to describe the pheno-
menology of this archetype, we shall have to consider all the aspects
which go to make up the total picture. For instance, in our analysis of
the *Timaeus*, we found that the number three represents an intellectual
schema only, and that the second mixture reveals the resistance of the
'recalcitrant fourth' ingredient, which we meet again as the 'adversary'
of the Christian Trinity. Without the fourth the three have no reality
as we understand it; they even lack meaning, for a 'thought' has
meaning only if it refers to a possible or actual reality. This relationship
to reality is completely lacking in the idea of the Trinity, so much so
that people nowadays tend to lose sight of it altogether, without
even noticing the loss. But we can see what this loss means when we are
faced with the problem of reconstruction – that is to say in all those
cases where the conscious part of the psyche is cut off from the unconscious part by a dissociation. This split can only be mended if consciousness is able to formulate conceptions which give adequate expression
to the contents of the unconscious. It seems as if the Trinity plus the
incommensurable 'fourth' were a conception of this kind. As part of the
doctrine of salvation it must, indeed, have a saving, healing, wholesome
effect. During the process of integrating the unconscious contents into
consciousness, undoubted importance attaches to the business of seeing
how the dream-symbols relate to trivial everyday realities. But, in a
deeper sense and on a long-term view, this procedure is not sufficient, as
it fails to bring out the significance of the archetypal contents. These
reach down, or up, to quite other levels than so-called common sense
would suspect. As *a priori* conditions of all psychic events, they are
endued with a dignity which has found immemorial expression in god-
like figures. No other formulation will satisfy the needs of the unconscious. The unconscious is the unwritten history of mankind from time
unrecorded. Rational formulae may satisfy the present and the immediate past, but not the experience of mankind as a whole. This calls for
the all-embracing vision of the myth, as expressed in symbols. If the
symbol is lacking, man's wholeness is not represented in consciousness.
He remains a more or less accidental fragment, a suggestible wisp of
consciousness, at the mercy of all the utopian fantasies that rush in to
fill the gap left by the totality symbols. A symbol cannot be made to
order as the rationalist would like to believe. It is a legitimate symbol
only if it gives expression to the immutable structure of the unconscious
and can therefore command general acceptance. So long as it evokes

belief spontaneously, it does not require to be understood in any other way. But if, from sheer lack of understanding, belief in it begins to wane, then, for better or worse, one must use understanding as a tool if the incalculable consequences of a loss are to be avoided. What should we then put in place of the symbol? Is there anybody who knows a better way of expressing something that has never yet been understood? [pp. 187-9]

Psychology and Religion, Collected Works, London, Routledge, 1958, vol. ii

In Arnold Toynbee we have the interesting case of a contemporary historian who starts with the 'decline and fall' attitude but whose multiple perspectives in the course of a long history make him turn to a very different view, expressed in images borrowed partly from biological science, partly from the psychologists' theory of types.

The work of Toynbee interests us particularly because his norm in assessing the Christian and other traditions remains always the ancient Hellenic philosophy and history, and so his work might well carry Porphyry's title, philosophos historia. It also shows how the whole course of an historical work is controlled by an initial preconception and value judgement. Toynbee works his long passage from the 'decline and fall' metaphor to a final view of the Church as 'a higher species of society'. His handling of evidence changes as his basic presupposition and metaphor change.

Toynbee would reject any attempt to solve a problem like that of philosophy and Christianity without extending the scale of reference. In his view history cannot envisage a smaller unit of study than the 'civilization'; so for him Church history on its own is impossible. A Church can only be understood in the setting of a civilization. Civilizations he argues, have their periods of organic genesis and growth, followed by breakdown and ultimate disintegration. As a civilization rises in response to the challenge of environment so its breakdown appears as a loss of command over environment; failure of self-determination becomes noticeable in intractability of institution and paralysis of creativity. Disintegration occurs at the stage when the civilization has become a 'universal state' and disintegration is largely due to a proletarian element of the universal society, representing an inner 'schism in the soul'. The proletariat of the universal state produces a universal Church which assumes the state 'installations', 'currencies' and 'corporations'. This Church in turn may become the matrix of another civilization. The historian therefore can view churches only in the context of civilizations.

Accordingly Toynbee sees in the rise of Christianity what he concludes to be a natural law among civilizations, namely that universal State tends to produce universal Church. A universal state's vision of itself as an urbs aeterna, *a city of God, always is an illusion. The state cannot be such an achieved end but only a means of service to some alien beneficiary, usually a universal religion which arises in its internal proletariat. The universal Church takes over the use and usufruct of the imperial* installations. *For example, the communication services and the roads now minister to the work of religious officials. The carefully sited imperial garrisons and colonies become focuses of missionary activity. The imperial provinces become the units of the Church's territorial administration. The capital cities of empire become 'seminaries' of the new religion. It is so with the various imperial* currencies. *For the official languages and alphabets of the empire become the Church's liturgical, theological and administrative vehicles. Imperial law produces canon law. The pagan calendar, inherited from a dim religious past and officially rationalized, is transmitted to the higher religion and there invested with a new sacrosanctity. Imperial monetary currency, of course, proves an obvious ally to the new Church. Use is also found for the imperial* corporations. *The basic one, the imperial army, is at first ostracized by the Church as idolatrous, but it finally teems with believers and supplies the Church's preaching with imagery derived from war. Similarly, the most important beneficiaries of the imperial civil service are neither successor states nor a further secular civilization, but the Church, whose key figures are recruits from the secular public service. And the political egalitarianism developed by imperial citizenship, in its dual types, municipal and oecumenical, forms the model for the ecclesiastical community local and catholic; so eventually 'believer' and 'citizen' become interchangeable terms.*

To the pagan champions of the universal state this assimilative activity of the Church naturally appears as a social disease.

10 ARNOLD TOYNBEE (1)

In entering now upon our study of universal churches we may find it convenient to start by examining their relation to the social environment in which they arise.

We have seen that a universal church is apt to come to birth during a Time of Troubles following the breakdown of a civilization, and to unfold itself within the political framework of a universal state which is the institutional manifestation of a temporary arrest in a broken-down civilization's decline and fall. Our study of universal states has brought out two facts about them: first that, in so far as their achievements bear fruit, the harvest is apt to be reaped, not by the sowers themselves, but by alien hands; and, second, that, in so far as they become creative in this indirect, second-hand, vicarious way, through the creative acts of their alien beneficiaries, they are creators unintentionally and indeed against their will. Their own primary aim is, not to be creative, but to survive, and the experience of losing their lives in order to find them again in the lives of their beneficiaries does not reconcile them to their fate; it provokes them to recalcitrance and indignation. Our survey in the preceding Part of this Study has shown that the principal benefici- aries of universal states are universal churches; and it is therefore not surprising that the champions of a universal state, at a stage in its history at which its own fortunes are manifestly on the wane, should dislike the spectacle of a universal church within its bosom profiting by services that the universal state is continuing to render without any longer being able to turn them to its own benefit. The church is therefore likely at first sight to wear the appearance of a social cancer; for in this situation and state of mind the universal state's devotees are apt, not merely to observe and resent the fact that the church is increasing while the state decreases, but to take it for granted that the beneficiary is also a parasite, and that the patent profit which it draws from its host is the cause of the host's malady. This diagnosis is as attractive as it is exacerbating; for it is always easier, both intellectually and morally, to debit one's ills to the account of some outside agency than to ascribe the responsibility to oneself.

In the decline of the Roman Empire an indictment of the Christian Church, which had been mounting up since the firing of the first telling shot by Celsus (*scribebat circa* A.D. 178), came to a head in the West when the Empire was in its death agonies there. An explosion of this hostile feeling was evoked in A.D. 416, in the heart of a 'die-hard' pagan Gallic devotee of Imperial Rome, by the sad sight of desert islands colonized – or, as Rutilius would have expressed it, infested – by Christian monks....

Rutilius's impersonal hostility towards the monks of Capraia was, however, a less painful feeling than the pang which, before his voyage was over, he was to suffer at the sadder sight of another island that had captivated a fellow countryman and acquaintance of the poet's own.... Through these lines there breathes the spirit of a still pagan aristocracy in the dissolving western provinces of the Roman Empire who saw the cause of the ruin of the body politic in the abandonment of the traditional worship of the Hellenic pantheon by pagan converts to

Christianity and in the suppression of Paganism by the Christian Emperor Theodosius.

This controversy between a sinking Roman Empire and a rising Christian Church raised an issue of such deep and general interest that it had stirred the feelings, not only of contemporaries directly concerned, but of a Posterity contemplating this historical spectacle across a great gulf of time and change. In the statement 'I have described the triumph of Barbarism and Religion', Gibbon not only sums up the seventy-one chapters of his book in nine words but proclaims himself a partisan of Celsus and Rutilius; and we can divine that, in his eyes, the cultural peak, as he saw it, of Hellenic history in the Antonine Age stood out clear across an intervening span of sixteen centuries which, for Gibbon, was a cultural trough. Out of the miry clay of this slough, the generation of Gibbon's grandfather in the Western World had tardily gained a footing on the slopes of another mountain, and from this point of vantage the twin peak was once again visible in all its majesty. 'On the morrow of the death of the Emperor Marcus,' we seem to hear Gibbon saying to himself, 'the Roman Empire, as I have described it in its glory, went into its decline. On the standards of value that I, Gibbon, and my kind in my world share with our kindred spirits in the world of Tacitus and Hadrian, a depreciation of values then set in, and this in every province of life. Religion and Barbarisim triumphed, and this lamentable state of affairs continued to prevail for hundreds and hundreds of dreary years, until only the other day, no longer ago than the close of the seventeenth century, a rational civilization began to emerge again.'

A Study of History, 12 volumes: Oxford, 1934–61, vol. vii. pp. 381–3

Toynbee, rejecting this hostile image of Church as social cancer, goes on to entertain the metaphor of 'chrysalis', the Church fostering a new civilization out of the decay of the old.

In the preceding chapter we have joined issue with Celsus and Rutilius and with the exponents of their thesis in our Western World in its modern age. We have contested the view that churches are cancers which eat the living tissues of a civilization away; yet we may still agree with Frazer's dictum, . . . that the tide of Christianity, which had flowed so strongly in the last phase of Hellenic history, had been ebbing in these latter days, and that the post-Christian Western Society that had emerged was one of the same order as the pre-Christian Hellenic Civilization. This observation opens up a second possible conception of the relation between universal churches and civilizations. On this view the churches present themselves, not as the sinister destroyers of civilizations, but as their useful humble servants. This role is assigned to the Catholic Christian Church – in contrast to the spirit of a gnostic form of Christianity that had gravitated towards the standpoint of the philosophies of Detachment – in a passage from the pen of a Modern Western scholar which has been quoted at a previous point in this Study without its significant concluding sentence.

'The old civilization was doomed, but this religious Nihilism puts nothing in its place. To the orthodox Christian, on the other hand, the Church stood, like Aaron, between the dead and the living, as a middle term between the things of the Next World and of This. It was the Body of Christ and therefore eternal; something worth living for and working for. Yet it was in the World as much as the Empire itself. The idea of the Church thus formed an invaluable fixed point, round which a new civilization could slowly crystallize.'

On this view, universal churches have their *raison d'être* in keeping the species of society known as civilizations alive by preserving a precious germ of life through the perilous interregnum between the dissolution of one mortal representative of the species and the genesis of another. In this repetitive process of the reproduction of civilizations, which is assumed to have an absolute value as an end in itself, the churches are useful and perhaps necessary, but secondary and transitional, phenomena. A church serves as egg, grub, and chrysalis between butterfly and butterfly. The writer of this Study had to confess that he, too, had been satisfied for many years with this rather patronizing view of the churches'role and nature; and he still believed that this conception of churches as chrysalises, unlike the conception of them as cancers, was true as far as it went; but he had come to believe that this was so small and unrepresentative a facet of the whole truth about universal churches as to be utterly misleading if it was mistaken for the whole of which it was in reality a minor part. It may be convenient at this point to explore, by an empirical survey, how far this partial truth – if such indeed it is – will carry us, and then to take the limit reached in this inquiry as a starting-point for seeking a standpoint that will yield a more enlightening perspective. . . .

. . . To investigate the process by which a new civilization does affiliate itself to a predecessor through the agency of a church, we must concentrate our attention on the living civilizations. On a synoptic view of the antecedents of these, we shall find ourselves able to analyse the process of transition to them from their predecessors into three phases which, from the standpoint of the chrysalis church, we may label 'conceptive', 'gestative', and 'parturient'.

The conceptive phase of the transmissionary role of a universal church sets in when the church seizes an opportunity that is offered to it by the secular social environment in which it arises.

This environment is the universal state which a disintegrating civilization throws up, at an advanced stage of its decline, in an effort to arrest the fatal process. By the time when this rally is achieved, and not least in the very act of achieving it, the ailing secular society, partly unintentionally and partly deliberately, has put out of action many of the master institutions of its phase of growth – above all, the parochial states which, while the society was still in health, gave such scope for variety in the exercise of its creative powers, and this not only in the political and economic fields, but in the visual arts, literature, and other provinces of culture. The universal state could not arise until its parochial predecessors had decimated their own ranks by recurrent fratricidal wars, and until the weakened survivors had exhausted their credit of affection and loyalty in the hearts of citizens on whom they had been calling for never-ceasing and ever-increasing sacrifices; and, after establishing itself, it could not secure its position against the threat of a recrudescence of international anarchy without curbing the remnant of parochial sovereignty and sapping the remnant of self-government. In this situation the sorely tried populations that have been united politically at last within the universal state's frontiers find themselves torn between conflicting feelings which they cannot reconcile. Their dominant emotions are a thirst for peace and quiet and a grateful acquiescence in the oecumenical régime that has brought them these long-desired blessings, and this general attitude of mind is the psychological foundation of the parvenu imperial government's rule. But the sense of relief is traversed and tempered by a sense of frustration; for Life cannot preserve itself by bringing itself to a halt; the stream of psychic energy known in the language of a Modern Western school of Psychology as *libido* continues to well up out of its springs in the subconscious depths; and, as the universal state settles down and its subjects begin to recuperate from their exhaustion, while the memory of the preceding Time of Troubles begins to fade, they suffer more and

F   133

more discomfort from the choking up of the ancient institutional outlets for the flow of the human 'social animal's' life-force.

This is a psychological need for which the universal state itself does not provide; for its *raison d'être* is the negative one of re-establishing control over destructive forces that have got out of hand; and, so far from being concerned to open up innocuous alternative channels for activity, it tends to look askance at all new manifestations of Life as so many more openings for fresh outbreaks of the demonic spirit of Anarchy. In this situation a nascent universal church may make its own fortune by doing for a stagnant secular society the service that is now its most urgent need; for it can open up new channels for the baulked spiritual energies of Mankind without asking the imperial government's leave and sometimes, still more effectively, in defiance of its veto. In the Roman Empire

> 'The victory of Christianity over Paganism . . . furnished the orator with new topics of declamation and the logician with new points of controversy. Above all, it produced a new principle, of which the operation was constantly felt in every part of Society. It stirred the stagnant mass from the inmost depths. It excited all the passions of a stormy democracy in the quiet and listless population of an overgrown empire. The fear of heresy did what the sense of oppression could not do; it changed men, accustomed to be turned over like sheep from tyrant to tyrant, into devoted partisans and obstinate rebels. The tones of an eloquence which had been silent for ages resounded from the pulpit of Gregory. A spirit which had been extinguished on the plains of Philippi revived in Athanasius and Ambrose.'

This passage from the pen of a Modern Western historian is as truthful as it is eloquent, but its theme is the second chapter in the story. At this stage the opening of new channels by the Christian Church did indeed release intellectual and political energies that had been dammed back so long that their currents had been flowing in reverse into the Dead Sea of Archaism. But this chapter followed a previous, and more critical, stage in the encounter between universal church and universal state in which a head-on collision between them had given ordinary men and women a fresh opportunity for making a supreme sacrifice that had been the glory and the tragedy of Society in the age of parochial sovereignty and fratricidal warfare.

Ibid, vol. vii, pp. 392–5

But Toynbee becomes discontent too with the idea of the higher religion acting as mere link between civilizations, and he finally decides to view religion as ultimate, and civilizations as simply overtures to it. 'Civilizations have forfeited their historical significance except in so far as they minister to the progress of religion.' Christianity is thus more than a temporary conductor between the decaying Hellenic civilization and that of the Western World. It is nothing less than a vital stage in the total spiritual development of humanity. Christianity assimilated the civic installations, currencies and corporations of the Roman Empire because of this larger destiny of superseding not only that civilization but perhaps the modern one as well. To the objection that Christianity up to our time has not manifested much effective progress to such a conquest Toynbee's answer would be: Wait and see! for twenty centuries is a relatively short time, not nearly long enough for the silt carried down from primitive origins to be purged from the stream of a higher religion. Evolution admittedly takes time. Toynbee's own thought takes a long time to evolve from the metaphor of 'cancer' to that of 'chrysalis' and finally to the rather Darwinian concept of religion as a 'higher species' of human society.

. . . The human beings who 'learnt through suffering' in the last agonies of the Sumeric and Egyptiac civilizations were precursors of Prophets of Israel and Judah who were enlightened, in their turn, by the tribulations of a Babylonic and Syriac Time of Troubles, and all these men of sorrows were precursors of Christ. The successive sufferings through which they won a progressive enlightenment stood out, on a retrospective view, as Stations of the Cross in anticipation of the Crucifixion.

In this perspective, Christianity could be seen to be the climax of a continuous upward movement of spiritual progress which had not merely survived successive secular catastrophes but had drawn from them its cumulative inspiration. To judge by this momentous historical instance, the circumstances favourable to spiritual and to secular progress are not only different but are antithetical; and this 'law' – if we have stumbled here upon a 'law' governing the relations between mundane life and Religion – is not a paradox. Spiritual and secular ideals are at variance; they are perpetually striving with one another for mastery over human souls; and it is therefore not surprising that souls should be deaf to the call of the Spirit in times of secular prosperity, and sensitive to the neglected whisper of the still small voice when the vanity of This World is brought home to them by secular catastrophes and when their hearts are softened by the sufferings and sorrows that these catastrophes inflict. When the house that Man has built for himself falls in ruin about his ears and he finds himself standing again in the open at the mercy of the elements, he also finds himself standing again face to face with a God whose perpetual presence is now no longer hidden from Man's eyes by prison walls of Man's own making. If this is the truth, the interregna which punctuate secular history by intervening between the submergence of one civilization and the emergence of a successor may be expected to have, as their counterparts in religious history, not breaches of continuity or pauses in the pulsation of life, but flashes of intense spiritual illumination and bursts of fervent spiritual activity. . . .

On this reading, the history of Religion appears to be unitary and progressive by contrast with the multiplicity and repetitiveness of the histories of civilizations; and this contrast in the Time-dimension presents itself in the Space-dimension as well; for Christianity and the other higher religions that, in the twentieth century of the Christian Era, were living side by side, in an *Oikoumenê* which had recently become coextensive with the whole habitable and traversable surface of the planet, had a closer affinity among themselves than coeval civilizations had been apt to have with one another.

Ibid. vol. vii, pp. 424–6

If the foregoing inquiry has convinced us that the churches embodying the higher religions are diverse approximate projections on Earth of one and the same *Civitas Dei*, and that the species of society of which this Commonwealth of God is the sole and unique representative is of a spiritually higher order than the species represented by the civilizations, we shall be encouraged to go farther in our experiment of inverting the assumption, on which we have tacitly proceeded in previous Parts of this Study, that, in the relation between churches and civilizations, the civilizations' role is dominant and the churches' role subordinate. Instead of dealing with churches in terms of civilizations, as hitherto, we shall boldly make the new departure of dealing with civilizations in terms of churches. If we are looking for a social cancer, we shall find it, not in a church which supplants a civilization, but in a civilization which supplants a church; and, if we have thought of a church as being a chrysalis through which one civilization reproduces itself in another, we shall now have to think, inversely, of the 'apparented' civilization in this genealogical series as being an overture to the epiphany of a church, and of the 'affiliated' civilization as being a regression from this higher level of spiritual attainment. . . .

If we take, as a test case for the verification of this thesis, the genesis of the Christian Church, and cite the tenuous yet significant evidence afforded by the transference of words from a secular to a religious meaning and usage, we shall find this philological testimony supporting the view that Christianity is a religious theme with a secular overture, and that this overture consisted, not merely in the Roman political achievement of an Hellenic universal state, but in Hellenism itself, in all its phases and aspects.

Ibid., vol. vii, 526–7

Toynbee's study of the past yields him a prophetic glimpse of the future. He sees the four contemporary higher religions of the world as 'variations on a single theme', which may yet harmonize. On this view all the declines and falls of civilizations have ministered to cumulative spiritual progress. Toynbee's history, then, like Augustine's, is a philosophy: he is always aware of the timeless transcending the historical process, always seeing temporal events sub specie aeternitatis, *seeing too the fitful religious progress of the past as a* praeparatio evangelica *for some higher spirituality to come.*

He thinks of inner spirit as prior to external achievement and as its mainspring. In this inner spirit man may realize a supra-temporal order, the City of God that transcends temporal civilization, and he is convinced that only this attention to the City of God can build the city of man. All this is not new to European thought. Toynbee has read it in William Temple, in Bossuet, above all in Augustine; he has even glimpsed its pagan philosophic origins in the Stoics and in Plato. It is a philosophia perennis, *the nearest thing we have, perhaps, to a unanimity of European wisdom.*

But Toynbee sees the future development as lying beyond traditional Mediterranean religion. For him a new universal religion would appear to be the future end-term of all the civilizations. This new spiritual fruition would come through a harmony of the Hellenic–Semitic synthesis with the higher religions that have taken over from the other main civilizations of the globe. This optimistic vision is based on a conviction of the spiritual equivalence of these extant higher religions, each ministering to a partial psychological need. To this view secular historians have voiced many objections, enough indeed to give Toynbee his material for a final volume of heart-searchings rather resembling Augustine's Retractationes. *His critics are generally unable to see events and civilizations and higher religions marching in uniform to such a well determined strategy; sometimes, too, they are unable to welcome his prospect of fideistic irrationality gaining the ultimate victory over the accumulated achievements of European intellect.*

11 H. R. TREVOR-ROPER

Such is Toynbee's new Dispensation. It is, of course, not entirely new; for Toynbee's whole system is by definition repetitive. Therefore this new Dispensation too has a historical precedent. The precedent is taken, as always, from Græco-Roman civilization. For although Toynbee claims to base his system on a number of past civilizations, in fact, as the critics have often pointed out, it is based on Græco-Roman civilization only – the only civilization which Toynbee has really studied and to whose pattern, as he interprets it, all other civilizations are now arbitrarily told to conform. So now the decline of the West must be made to resemble the decline of Greece and Rome, and the new universal Church, of which Toynbee is the prophet, must resemble the old Christian Church, in the days when it was new. The wheel of history has once again come full circle. The future is once again made clear by the past.

For did not the ancient pagan civilization of the Hellenic world, obedient to the Toynbeean Laws, duly decompose? Were not its political forms – the independent Greek cities, the Hellenistic monarchies, the Roman republic itself – utterly extinguished? Did not the memory of its poets and philosophers happily fade away, burnt out of human recollection by the purifying fires of clerical bigotry, until the rot of the Renaissance allowed them to return? But did not the more essential parts of that civilization, its mysteries and mummeries, its sacraments and sacrifices, Isis and Adonis and Mithras, happily survive, gathered up and preserved in that new syncretist religion, 'that quaint Alexandrian *tutti-frutti*,' as Norman Douglas once described it, Christianity? Even so, Toynbee tells us, our Western civilization is now fast decomposing. We shall be conquered, destroyed, absorbed. Our political forms, our liberties, our culture shall be crushed out. But what of that? For our religious beliefs, which alone matter, will be preserved, pickled as one of the ingredients of a new syncretist religion, a new *tutti-frutti*, 'a mish-mash', as one commentator has described it, 'of the Virgin Mary and Mother Isis, of St Michael and Mithras, of St Peter and Muhammad, of St Augustine and Jalal-ad-Din Mawlana'. Such, we are now assured, is to be the new 'universal religion' which will render political conquest a positive boon and will replace for all mankind the use of human reason and the remembrance of its great landmarks, the Renaissance, the Reformation, the New Philosophy, the Enlightenment.

'Arnold Toynbee's Millennium', *Encounter* 8, June 1957, p. 20

Toynbee, in spite of his dependence on the basic European heritage, has doubts as to whether his prophetic history could be labelled Christian. His doubts are natural. A Christian history has to be theological. It was so, we noted, in the earliest Christian documents, the New Testament, where the events recorded were seen as the actions of God to which all secular matters were subordinate. The early Fathers adhered to this conception. The Apologists made it clear that the Greek philosophy in which they had been educated could be no more than the domestic servant of their new faith. The Church never saw herself as dominated by the pagan culture. She could profess a use of it as occasion and controversy demanded, but the whole development of Hellenic civilization was in her eyes but the ground-clearing propaedeutic for her own teaching (praeparatio evangelica). Apologetic writers have always continued to follow this line of argument, saying that the paganism old or new opposing Christianity is junior to its rival in thought and morality. If hostile, they call paganism demonic; if sympathetic, they declare that at best it is but a prelude to the more developed thing; so that as long as it persists into the Christian age it persists as something superseded, a relic, a mode passée. In either case they start from the theological axiom that the birth of Christianity was a unique historical event.

Likewise the Christian style of history cannot easily regard all extant higher religions as equivalently final. It is a common view of Protestant missionaries, and finds theological support in the writings of Barth and his follower Kraemer, that there is a radical distinction between the Christian Gospel and all other religions; these can have at best only a relative validity, and the similarities that are conducive to praeparatio evangelica do not cancel the radical otherness of Christianity and the perception of a certain demonic character in alien religions. This leaves the corollary that future spiritual progress can never come by Toynbee's ultimate syncretism but only by Christian conversion of the heathen. In this perspective we find a modern view of extant higher religions comparable to the attitude of early Church Fathers to pagan thought.

12 MARTIN WIGHT

The Christian critic will read the whole of this Part with sympathy and admiration, above all for the comprehensive charity with which you endeavour to see all the Higher Religions *sub specie aeternitatis*. But he may well have misgivings about your main arguments, and believe that you do not maintain the full tension inherent in the Christian problem of comparative religion. It is convenient to sum up some criticisms at this point.

1. Your description of Christianity is philosophical rather than historico-theological, 'Hellenic' rather than 'Hebraic'. You define Christianity in terms of the assertion that 'God is Love', or as 'unique in revealing God to Man as Man's father and brother'. But this is only true as far as it goes, and it does not go far enough. The central declaration of Christianity is not that God *is* something, but that God *has done* something; it is Hebraic first and Hellenic second; its uniqueness is primarily historico-theological, and only consequentially theologico-philosophical. God *has done* something in history; He has acted *in history* to show the meaning of history. . . .

The Christian reader misses, in your account of Christianity, this insistence upon its springing from a unique and particular historical event which is charged with eschatological significance, and upon its therefore providing, alone among the Higher Religions except Islam, and far more fully than Islam, an answer to the question of the meaning of History.

2. It follows upon this that the Christian critic may think that you misrepresent the relationship between Christianity and Judaism, and consequently misrepresent Judaism itself. . . .

. . . Where Christianity does seem to 'break decisively' with Judaism is not in its proclamation of Love, nor in its exclusiveness, but in its universality. It was not simply, as you say, 'an intervention of God Himself to redeem the Jews of Jesus' day'. In the Synoptic tradition no less than in John there is a clear refusal to limit the sphere of the call of God. The Old Israel which was limited to the seed of Abraham is superseded by the New Israel which embraces all who will repent and believe: the nature of the Christian Revelation is such that its promise and its claims are universal. But here again the discontinuity with Judaism is only superficial, for Judaism, inasmuch as it was an abortive Higher Religion, was also potentially universalist, and the Prophets had foretold the bringing of God's salvation to the Gentiles.

3. The apparent under-estimation of the exclusiveness and universality of Christianity (the Christian critic might continue) throws your comparison of Christianity with the other Higher Religions out of focus. The inquiry necessarily begins from the assumption of the comparability of the Higher Religions, but the assumption is not sufficiently re-examined in the course of the discussion. . . .

. . . There is no reason *a priori* to suppose that the 'fully-fledged Higher Religions . . . derived from the secondary civilizations' are the collective final term in the history of Religion. Nor is any evidence or argument produced for your assertion that it is their 'destiny . . . that they should all become world-wide without conflicting with one another' except for the theory that they correspond to Jung's psychological types; and this (fascinating, illuminating, and important as it is) cannot be more than a 'rationalization' of a particular historical constellation.

. . . Indeed, it is surely plain that the present constellation of Higher Religions is due not to psychological typology but to that much wider thing (in which psychological typology may play its part) which we can only call cultural history. The psychological theory could only be upheld if it could be shown that there is a numerical predominance of each psychological type in the region of the World where its 'corresponding' Higher Religion has the ascendancy, and for this there is no evidence whatever. It is just as likely that the Higher Religions mould psychology as that 'each of them may correspond and minister to one of the psychological types into which Human Nature appears to be differentiated', or, in a word, as that psychology determines the Higher Religions.

4. You admit the concept of a *praeparatio evangelica* throughout in your interpretation of Judaism, and in your account of Paganism, though you only use the phrase itself twice, I think, *en passant*. But from the Christian point of view it is the fundamental principle for explaining the relationship between Christianity and other religions, and for reconciling their truths and insight with the exclusive claims of the Christian Revelation, and the Christian critic may wish that you had developed it more thoroughly. It is expressed in the quotation from Temple, and it could be expressed in the very fine metaphor of

the veils which you use in a different connexion. (It is magnificently stated in the passage from Bevan's *Jerusalem under the High Priests* which you quote in V. vi. 132: a passage which not only states the purpose and scope of the *praeparatio*, but also emphasizes the uniqueness and transcendence of That which was prepared for.) The *praeparatio evangelica* was recognized from the earliest days of the Church, especially by St Paul, when he preached at Athens, and in his acknowledgement of the validity of Natural Law among the Gentiles. In the second century A.D. the conception was elaborated, first of all, of course, to explain the relations between Christianity and Judaism, by St Irenaeus in answer to Marcion, but also, more tentatively, to explain the relations between Christianity and Paganism, by St. Justin and Clement of Alexandria. . . .

5. But there has always been a tension in the relationship of Christianity with other religions: a tension between apprehending them as a *praeparatio evangelica* and apprehending them as obstacles to the spreading of the Gospel. This tension reflects the inherent ambiguity of other religions, which are at the same time both 'precursors' and 'adversaries'; and it springs from the essential nature of a revelation which is at once exclusive and universal, which proclaims itself as Truth among partial truths and falsehoods, which make absolute claims and knows (in a sense) that they will be rejected, which is a light shining in a darkness that has not comprehended it. . . .

Perhaps the most that can be said about the history of this tension in the Christian attitude to other religions is that, as Christianity has become less concerned with primitive religions of the kind that it superseded in the Roman Empire and has become more concerned with the other Higher Religions, so its emphasis has shifted from apprehension of the demonic character of other religions to recognition of their *praeparatio evangelica*. But this, once again, has taken place within the abiding framework of tension, of a 'dramatic' relationship, because these spring from the very nature of spiritual life and of Christianity itself. Now, as always, Christianity comes not only to fulfil, but also to purge. . . .

6. For these reasons the Christian critic will, I think, be dissatisfied with your handling of 'the crux for an historian brought up in the Christian tradition', and will hold that your solution of the problem of the relationship between Christianity and the other Higher Religions fails to be in Christian terms. He will be able to accept neither your

premiss of the spiritual equivalence of the Higher Religions derived from the secondary civilizations nor the conclusion, to which it inevitably leads, that they have a common destiny. He will note that in due course you qualify your assumption by tentatively suggesting a spiritual deficiency in the Indic religions which has led to an apparently inconsistent assimilation to Christianity; but it will seem to him that in the end, with your argument of the 'harmony' or 'symphony' of the Higher Religions, you yourself capitulate to a Hindu mode of thought. . . .

Protestants see the development of the Church in federal rather than unitary terms as the propagation of autonomous and self-propagating indigenous churches. Indeed, the reason why Protestants of the Reformed tradition would hesitate to accept the quotation from Karl Adam with the substitution of 'Christianity' for 'Catholicism' is because of the belief that the Roman Catholic theory of the development of doctrine compromises the purity of the original κήρυγμα and that Roman Catholicism already goes too far in the direction of syncretism. But this issue between the Roman Catholic Church, the members of the World Council of Churches, and the Moscow Patriarchate, which together compose the Christian World today (which is also an issue *within* each church, as it was between Matteo Ricci and Clement XI, who finally condemned his methods) is nothing compared with their common distance from your own conclusion. For it is a debate within the common ground of conviction that the Church (however defined, and whatever its proper methods) is in the World to redeem it and that its *raison d'être* is to convert all nations. Paul's doctrine of the gathering of the Gentiles is only a development of Christ's own declaration of the oecumenical character of his mission, and is foreshadowed, in simpler terms, by the Prophets' vision of an ultimate day in which all the World will acknowledge the God of Israel. . . .

But, while he will disagree with so much that you say, the Christian critic will be deeply grateful to you for this Part, because it will appear to him that, just as you have abandoned your original judgement that all civilizations are philosophically equivalent and have found that 'civilizations . . . have ceased to constitute intelligible fields of study for us and have forfeited their historical significance except in so far as they minister to the progress of Religion', so the suppressed logic of your argument (rather than the weight of your evidence) drives on towards discarding your assumption that all higher religions are spiritually equivalent, and to the conclusion that the higher religions in their turn cease to be intelligible fields of study and forfeit their historical significance except in so far as they are related to Christianity.

'The Crux for an Historian brought up in the Christian Tradition', *Annex* to A. J. Toynbee, *A Study of History*, vol. vii, pp. 737–48

There are times, however, when Toynbee comes very near to a Christian statement. He uses the Augustinian term, Civitas Dei, to emphasize that only the religious sense of a higher than human presence in the cosmos will effectively unite all men in brotherhood, and that without it the most rational socialist ideals will fail.

13 ARNOLD TOYNBEE (2)

Christians believe – and a study of History assuredly proves them right – that (beyond the narrow circle of the tribe, in which a parochial 'honour among thieves' is maintained at the prohibitive moral price of an Ishmaelitish warfare against a world of foreign enemies) the brotherhood of Man is impossible for Man to achieve in any other way than by enrolling himself as a citizen of a *Civitas Dei* which transcends the human world and has God himself for its king. And any one who holds this belief will feel certain, *a priori*, that the Marxian excerpt from a Christian Socialism is an experiment which is doomed to failure because it has denied itself the aid of the spiritual power. . . .

A Study of History, vol. v, p. 585

However distasteful Toynbee's essay in universal history may be to some Christians, his gallant attempt at integral understanding is fresh and illuminating. The historian whose sympathy is confined to Europe will miss the insight that comes from such comparison with cultures alien to his own. Christian history will henceforth be open to criticism if it does not, in Simone Weil's words, stand at the intersection of the Christian with the non-Christian.

The opening of minds to wider sympathies than hitherto is perhaps a feature of our time. Even Catholic Christians, hitherto proverbially conservative, seem willing nowadays to follow Toynbee in his accommodating attitude to other spiritualities, even if this involves an unusual risk of syncretism. Their increased sympathy is manifest, even if the Catholic Church may never officially canonize Arnold Toynbee as its futuristic Eusebius!

His outlook is based on a Greek philosophic ideal elaborated by the Stoics, that of the brotherhood of man, still unattained in our own day and still hoped for. Toynbee believes that the ideal cannot be attained by humanist rationalism alone but by rationalism allied with a new religious faith that has emerged from its merely local, tribe-like, allegiances and become truly catholic.

History, secular or religious, can contribute to this ideal through its comparative perspectives that enlarge human sympathy. Even within a set tradition it can contribute to tolerance from its ability to analyse ideology genetically, aiding discernment of what is essential and what adventitious. In this it may well serve religious reformers of the future, indicating to them even further extensions of the historic process we have been considering: the praeparatio evangelica *whereby philosophic rationalism was conscripted to serve under the standard of a Galilean peasant.*

14 CHARLES PÉGUY

Les rêves de Platon avaient marché pour lui
Du cachot de Socrate aux prisons de Sicile.
Les soleils idéaux pour lui seul avaient lui,
Et pour lui seul chanté le gigantesque Eschyle.

Les règles d'Aristote avaient marché pour lui
Du cheval d'Alexandre aux règles scholastiques.
Et pour lui l'ascéticisme et la règle avaient lui
Des règles d'Epicure aux règles monastiques.

'La Gréce', *Cahiers de la Quinzaine*, xv, 4; Paris, 28 December 1913

For him the dreams of Plato had made their way/From the cell of Socrates to Sicilian jails./The ideal suns had shone for him alone,/For him had Aeschylus of the giants sung.//The rules of Aristotle had marched for him/From the horse of Alexander to the schoolmen's rules./For him alone asceticism and rule had shone/From the rules of Epicurus to the monastic rules.

Sources Quoted

Philosophic

HERACLITUS of Ephesus (*c*. 500 B.C.), most impressive of the 'Ionian' philosophers, conceived the universe in terms of change and conflict, and human wisdom as consciousness of order generated by conflict. Man can 'neither say nor conceal but only indicate' this wisdom.

PARMENIDES (*c*. 450 B.C.) of Elea, 'Italian' philosopher who wrote a long poem wherein a goddess philosopher expounds monism. Diversity, she says, exists only in name. She bases philosophy on logical method and, although herself divine, is careful to distinguish rational thought from mere belief.

EURIPIDES (*c*. 485–407 B.C.), youngest of the three great Greek tragedians, nineteen of whose ninety-two plays survive. They are more experimental and uneven in character than those of either Aeschylus or Sophocles; they follow the civic convention of adhering to religious mythology only to exploit this material for new purposes, portraying psychology, patriotism, romance. Affected by the interests of the sophist philosophers the plays appear to be on the side of the new enlightenment rather than traditional theology.

ISOCRATES (436–338 B.C.), Athenian speech-writer and educationalist. He criticized the teaching of superficial technique practised by other rhetoricians and regarded his own rhetoric as a creative process or 'philosophy'. Nevertheless Plato in his condemnation of rhetoric as a meretricious art seems to have included Isocrates as being too empirical and 'unphilosophic'.

PLATO (429–347 B.C.), disciple of Socrates, most famous of the Greek philosophers, fountain-head of European thought and prose style.

ARISTOTLE (384–322 B.C.), Plato's most brilliant pupil. His school treatises after being introduced by Boethius to the Latin West and by Leontius to the Greek Church, dominated medieval Christian thought as Plato had dominated the patristic era.

PHILODEMUS (first century B.C.), an Epicurean. Some charred papyri of his works were recovered in excavation from a Roman library at Herculaneum which was buried by the lava of Vesuvius in the famous eruption of A.D. 79. The fragments include a popular history of philosophy.

PLUTARCH (c. A.D. 46–120), the famous Greek-born biographer of ancient personalities, compiled about sixty treatises on a variety of topics, moral philosophy predominating. Richness of quotation makes him a valuable source book. It is a telling reflection on the division between educated and uneducated classes in his day that despite his comprehensive social observations he never noticed Christianity.

PHILO (c. 20 B.C.–c. A.D. 50) of Alexandria, voluminous philosopher-exegete and most famous of the Hellenist Jews. By adopting the concept of *logos* and by the use of allegory he was able to unite philosophic notions with scriptural. Mystic and Platonist, he stressed divine transcendence. Study of his work by Clement, Origen and Plotinus made his ideas and methods a basis of Christian theology.

MARCUS AURELIUS (A.D. 121–80), Stoic Roman Emperor. Concerned as much with the moral as with the military defence of the Empire he wrote down brief meditations during his frontier campaigns, but punished Christians for their aloofness from imperial religion. Several Christian 'Apologies' were addressed to him.

SEXTUS EMPIRICUS (second century A.D.), a physician who favoured 'empirical' medicine rather than that influenced by philosophical theories such as teleology. Philosophically he was a Sceptic, and his writings are valuable as the best extant account of ancient scepticism. They are: *Outlines of Pyrrhonism*, *Against the Dogmatists*, and *Against the Professors* (*Adversus Mathematicos*).

PTOLEMY (second century A.D.), astronomer, geographer and mathematician. His encyclopedia of astronomy, *The Greater* (*megiste*) *Collection* became the Almagest of the Arabs and solidly imposed its geocentric universe on the medieval mind, until Gemistos Plethon drew attention to Strabo.

GALEN (c. A.D. 130–c. 200), after Hippocrates the best known medical authority of the ancient world, author of about 400 treatises. He was Aristotelian and monotheist and believed that God's laws can be discerned through research. God works by law, but not by miracle: 'In this we differ from Moses.'

Hermetica (first to third century A.D.), a group of philosophic-religious writings ascribed to 'Hermes Thrice-greatest', Hellenized equivalent of the Egyptian god Thoth. They contain a mystic doctrine of deification through *gnosis*, supported by a fusion of Platonic, Stoic, Pythagorean, and non-Hellenic, even Jewish, elements. The first treatise, *Poimandres*, has an account of the astral ascent of the soul to God. These tracts when discovered in the eleventh century by Psellos entered the Platonism of the Renaissance.

DIOGENES LAERTIUS (third century A.D.), a type of the later Greek scholasticism, wrote a biographical history of Greek philosophy, in 'lives, opinions and sayings'. Though gossipy and unscientific, for some thinkers such as Epicurus it is almost our only extant record.

PLOTINUS (A.D. *c.* 205–70), the last great name in ancient pagan philosophy. A pupil of the Alexandrian master, Ammonius Saccas, he came to Rome and founded his own school there in 244. His writings were edited by his pupil Porphyry into six groups of nine chapters (*enneades*). Uniting the rationalist and irrationalist Greek traditions, Plotinus is an intellectual mystic. Reality, in his Platonic view, means emanation from an incomprehensible unity or first principle into thought and life, below which is the realm of matter. Personal human life is a separation from universal life and must be recalled by ascetic discipline beyond sensation and intellect to an ecstatic 'feeling' of the primal unity. Through writers like Dionysius and Augustine his Platonism affected Christian spirituality very deeply.

PORPHYRY (A.D. 233–*c.* 304) a Hellenist Syrian who became the most devoted pupil and biographer of Plotinus and reduced to readable order his master's illegible writings. A great polymath, trained in mathematics and logic, he made a critical study of popular religion, including Christianity, and of the current practices of theurgy and magic and oracle-collecting. He studied Aristotle, probably as propaedeutic to Plotinian Platonism, and parts of this study when translated into Latin by Boethius set the cadre and style of medieval scholasticism. His greatest work, *Against the Christians*, was banned and burnt; only fragments of it survive.

EUNAPIUS (A.D. *c.* 345–*c.* 414), a rhetorician whose *Lives of the Philosophers* is a useful source on Neoplatonist teachers. In his life of the professor Maximus he describes Christianity as a 'fabulous and formless darkness', a phrase which gave the poet Yeats one of his memorable lines.

PROCLUS (A.D. 410–85), Neoplatonist successor (*diadochos*) of Plato as head of the Athenian Academy, a great systematizer and commentator. Some of his *Elements of Theology* was translated into Latin in the twelfth century under the title *Liber de Causis*.

SIMPLICIUS was among the Athenian philosophers displaced by Justinian's closure in A.D. 529 of the pagan Platonic Academy. After two years as a refugee in Persia he returned to Greece and wrote commentaries on Aristotle which aimed in Neoplatonic style to reconcile Plato with his pupil.

Christian

Gospels, the writings that record sayings and actions of Jesus, four of which were canonized by the Church as orthodox. Of the others that survive some probably contain authentic elements, others are tales of popular fancy. Some were compiled with Gnostic interests in mind, such as the *Gospel of Thomas*, Greek fragments of which were among the early papyrus discoveries in Egypt; more recently a complete Coptic translation has come to light. No known Gospel was written out of purely historical interest. Oral tradition was largely relied on as source, and also perhaps personal revelations whereby 'the Word of the Lord came to' prophetic believers.

Septuagint, the pre-Christian Greek translation of the Hebrew Old Testament, which was accepted into the Christian Bible. The translation was attributed by Hellenistic Jewish legend to seventy inspired translators summoned to Alexandria by Ptolemy II (288–247 B.C.). Much of the work adheres to a pious and pedantic literalism. There are some notable inaccuracies and even a few traces of Greek mythology in it. It was the text used by the earliest Christian Church, as can be gathered from the textual accuracy of New Testament quotations from it.

JUSTIN (*c.* 100–*c.* 165) best known of the Christian Apologists, after exploring various philosophies became a Christian. He addressed two defences of Christianity to Roman Emperors. Though not deeply philosophic he did try to initiate a dialogue between Christianity and pagan philosophy, relying on the Stoic notion of cosmic generative reason and on the Platonic notion of divine transcendence. Some second- and third-century treatises (*Discourse to the Greeks, Exhortation to the Greeks, The Monarchy of God*) were falsely attributed to him.

ATHENAGORAS (second century) wrote an Apologia to the Emperor Marcus Aurelius and his son, seeking to refute pagan calumnies about Christian 'atheism' and incest. He put his case in a lucid style modelled on Plato and also started the habit of borrowing Platonic terms to fix Christian ideas.

HIPPOLYTUS (*c.* 170–*c.* 236), though a presbyter of the Church of Rome wrote, and apparently preached, in Greek. He was a bitter critic of contemporary bishops of Rome. His *Refutation of All Heresies* begins by describing the main Greek philosophies and then goes on to show that the chief Christian heresies are built out of them. But his own doctrine of two kinds of *logos*, one eternal and the other temporal, was regarded by the Roman bishops as a danger to monotheism.

IRENAEUS (*c.* 130–*c.* 200), bishop of Lyons, wrote in Greek a 'refutation of all heresies' and of 'so called gnosis'. The work survives mainly in a Latin version. Unlike Clement of Alexandria he did not present Christianity as a philosophic gnosis, but stressed the practical discipline of the Church, the episcopate and tradition.

CLEMENT of Alexandria (*c.* 150–*c.* 215), possibly a native of Athens, succeeded Pantaenus as head of the Alexandrian theological school (*didaskaleion*), a Hellenistic institution where both Christian faith and the profane disciplines were taught. He wrote *An Exhortation to the Greeks* (*Protreptikos*), *The Tutor* (*Paidagogos*) and *Miscellanies* (*Stromateis*).

ORIGEN (*c.* 185–*c.* 254), pupil and successor of Clement in the Catechetical school of Alexandria. He had studied under the Alexandrian pagan philosopher Ammonius Saccas, probably with Plotinus as his companion. His voluminous writings cover biblical criticism, theology and asceticism. His *De Principiis* is the first Christian theological work which breathes the authentic spirit and precision of ancient philosophy; because of its suspected orthodoxy the whole Greek text has not managed to survive, though much of it has been laboriously reconstructed from quotations and from two early Latin translations. His other notable writing on our topic is the apologetic treatise *Contra Celsum*, which fortunately preserves much of Celsus's philosophic attack on the exclusive claims of the Church, on its biblical miracles and its dogmas, and on its refusal to support the state. Though Origen may fairly get credit for being the founder of Christian systematic theology he was in later ages one of its most maligned exponents.

EUSEBIUS (*c.* 260–340) bishop of Caesarea, the first great Church historian, who recorded the period from the Apostles to Constantine. His adulatory *Biography of Constantine* is witness to the changed relations of Church and State in the new Christian Empire. His *Demonstration of the Gospel* and *Preparation of the Gospel* (in fifteen books) argue the superiority of Christianity and the Scriptures over Greek culture, but allow the latter a propaedeutic value.

NEMESIUS (*c.* 300), bishop of Emesa in Syria. His treatise *On Human Nature* is written in genuinely philosophic terms while still agreeing with the tenets of Christian faith. It relies much on medical information.

BASIL (*c.* 330–379), brother of Gregory of Nyssa, was a companion of Gregory of Nazianzus and of the Emperor Julian during their studies at Athens. The rules he evolved in his monastic practice became basic in later Greek asceticism. His numerous letters illustrate social life in the Christian Empire. He was appointed bishop of Caesarea in 370 and this involved him in the defence of orthodoxy against the Arian monotheism of Eunomius, a bishop who taught that there is one supreme absolute essence or ungenerated intellect, out of which the Son is generated, as the Holy Spirit is from the Son; this rather abstract Platonic trinitarianism had made Eunomius critical of visible symbols and sacraments and ecclesiastical practices.

GREGORY of Nazianzus (329–89) studied with Basil at the pagan university of Athens and like him became a monk. He wrote theological addresses and compiled, with Basil, a selection from the works of Origen (*Philokalia*).

GREGORY of Nyssa (*c.* 330–*c.* 395) brother of Basil, chief of the bishops who upheld the orthodox creed, which had been formulated at Nicaea (325) against Arius, during the Council of Constantinople in 381. His numerous sermons, biblical commentaries, and ascetic exhortations show acquaintance with Platonism. The two Gregorys and Basil make up the patristic group known as the Cappadocian Fathers.

JOHN CHRYSOSTOM (*c.* 347–407) patriarch of Constantinople, the most prolific of the Greek Fathers (*PG*, volumes 47–64). Educated at Antioch both in theology and, under the orator Libanius, in pagan literature, he emulates Attic oratory with his imaginative style, relatively free from Semitic intrusions. He is not very philosophic, and he follows the Alexandrian habit of employing allegory to intellectualize the Scriptures.

CYRIL (d. 444), patriarch of Alexandria and opponent of philosophers, championed Trinitarian orthodoxy in the stormy wake of the condemned Arian heresy. His views were embodied in the dogmas of the famous Councils of Ephesus (431) and Chalcedon (451). Nevertheless his unguarded use of the Aristotelian word for 'nature' (*physis*) as if it were roughly synonymous with 'person' (*hypostasis*) gave some of his most pious followers occasion for starting the persistent schism of Monophysitism, teaching that there is but one nature, as one person, in Christ.

SYNESIUS of Cyrene (*c.* 370–414), a remarkable case of Hellenist survival. Of aristocratic pagan family, he was chosen by popular acclaim to become bishop of Ptolemais. Though as yet unbaptized, he decided to accept this influential post, having made up his mind to go on being a *philosophos* in private, holding theories of the pre-existence of the soul and the eternity of the world, and regarding the biblical stories as myths. His letters and the work called *Dion* show that the life of philosophic learning was more congenial to him than religious faith or asceticism.

BOETHIUS (*c.* 480–524), Roman aristocrat, held the office of chief minister under the Ostrogothic usurper of the Western Empire, Theodoric, who executed him on a suspicion of treason. Like Synesius he was an ardent Hellenist, and though certain theological treatises in Aristotelian idiom are now certainly accepted as his, proving him a Christian, his final masterpiece, *The Consolation of Philosophy*, is entirely a product of the Greek Platonic tradition, whose main theses it transmitted to the Middle Ages, Latin and Greek.

DIONYSIUS (*c.* 500), the pseudo-Areopagite, is the name given to the author of certain mystical writings which combine Neoplatonic ideas, particularly that of the hierarchical nature of reality, with Christianity. They speak of mystic union (*henosis*) with God, achieved by an advancing process of deification (*theiosis*) which supersedes sense and intellect. These writings were at an early stage attributed to the Dionysius of *Acts* 17. 34, and so enjoyed sub-apostolic authority in the Middle Ages; they were translated into Latin by John Eriugena. Doubts of their authenticity were raised at the Renaissance and were never hushed, though the Abbé Migne as late as 1886 still placed them at the hallowed beginnings of his Greek Patrology (*PG*, vol. 3–4). In 1895 Stiglmayr detected their heavy borrowings from the pagan Neoplatonist, Proclus, and so brought their ancient prestige to an end.

JUSTINIAN (483–565), Roman Emperor resident at Constantinople, sought to reunite the Eastern and Western parts of the harassed Empire, then politically and religiously divided. He is renowned for his buildings, especially the Byzantine Hagia Sophia, for his illiberal closure of the ancient Platonic school of Athens in 529, and for his codification of the Roman Law, comprising *Codex*, *Novellae* (additional constitutions), *Digest* (juristic extracts) and *Institutes* (a textbook of law).

JOHN of Damascus (*c.* 675–*c.* 749), of wealthy Christian family residing in Islamic territory, became a monk near Jerusalem. A fellow-monk urged him to write his tripartite *Fountain of Knowledge*, dealing with dialectic, heresy and orthodox faith. The philosophic part is distinctly Aristotelian; it had a profound influence on later Greek theology.

Barlaam and Joasaph (possibly eleventh century), a much repeated medieval romance about the conversion of a young Indian prince, Joasaph or Josaphat, by a Christian hermit, Barlaam. It was traditionally attributed, with little or no textual or palaeographical justification, to Saint John of Damascus. The work has recently been identified as a

Christian version of the story of the Buddha's renunciation, 'Josaphat' standing for 'Bodisaf' the young Buddha. Both prince and hermit are to be found as saints in the Latin Church calendar – a distinction which the Buddha even in his most enlightened moments could scarcely have expected!

PHOTIUS (c. 810–891), patriarch of Constantinople, though his life was disturbed by dispute and schism (867) with Rome, was a man of encyclopaedic learning. His massive *Bibliotheke*, a record of books read, is a mine of information about ancient books accessible to him but no longer to us.

PSELLOS (c. 1019–c. 1078) is an instance of the Renaissance spirit at work remarkably early and outside Italy. In 1045 he was made professor of philosophy at the revived university of Constantinople. At a time when scholasticism had yet to capture the West Psellos was already devoting himself to 'reopening the well-spring' of ancient Platonism. In the polymath style of the later Greek tradition he wrote on a large variety of topics, including a history of his own times and theology of strongly anti-Latin flavour. His Platonism brought back Proclus and other late Platonist writers who had been neglected by the ecclesiastical Aristotelians.

GEMISTUS PLETHON (c. 1355–1450) is the chief Renaissance product of the Neoplatonism revived by Michael Psellos. His visit to the Council of Florence in 1439 imported to the West his enthusiasm for Plato and was a turning point in the fortunes of Latin Aristotelianism. As with some of the earlier Neoplatonists we have noted, his Christian interests were completely subordinated to his philosophy, which is distinctly pagan and shows the persistence of the ancient rationalism. This 'religion of philosophy', bitterly dissatisfied with the contemporary Christian asceticism, advocated a more drastic Reformation than any ever suggested in the West: a supersession of both Christian and Islamic faith by return to 'natural' religion.

Further Reading

F. M. CORNFORD, *From Religion to Philosophy*. Cambridge University Press, 1912; Harper Torchbook, 1957

W. JAEGER, *The Theology of the Early Greek Philosophers*, trans. E. S. Robinson. Oxford University Press, 1947
— *Paideia: The Ideals of Greek Culture*, trans. Gilbert Highet. Oxford University Press, 1943–5

C. H. DODD, *The Bible and the Greeks*. London, Hodder & Stoughton, 1935

W. FAIRWEATHER, *Jesus and the Greeks*. Edinburgh, T. and T. Clark, 1924

J. M. CAMPBELL, *The Greek Fathers*. New York, 1963

A. H. ARMSTRONG and R. A. MARKUS, *Christian Faith and Greek Philosophy*. London, Darton, 1960

W. JAEGER, *Early Christianity and Greek Paideia*. Harvard University Press, 1962

A. WIFSTRAND, *L'église ancienne et la culture grecque*, trans. L.-M. Dewailly. Paris, 1962

E. HATCH, *The Influence of Greek Ideas on Christianity*. London 1888; Harper Torchbook, 1957.

The reader who desires to pursue the issue beyond the threshold of our present little anthology will find that the last mentioned work with its new bibliography in the Harper edition by F. C. Grant is an admirable stimulant to *historia*. For information on editions of the sources he can consult *The Oxford Classical Dictionary* and *The Oxford Dictionary of the Christian Church*.

Index